Bra

Bra

A THOUSAND YEARS OF STYLE, SUPPORT AND SEDUCTION

STEPHANIE PEDERSEN

David & Charles

A DAVID & CHARLES BOOK

David & Charles is a subsidiary of F+W (UK) Ltd.,
and F+W Publications Inc. company

First published in the UK in 2004
Copyright © Studio Cactus 2004

Distributed in North America
by F+W Publications, Inc.
4700 East Galbraith Road
Cincinnati, OH 45236
1-800-289-0963

A catalogue record for this book is available
from the British Library.

ISBN 0 7153 2067 X

Printed in Singapore by Star Standard
for David & Charles
Brunel House   Newton Abbot   Devon

Visit our website at
www.davidandcharles.co.uk

David & Charles books are available from all
good bookshops; alternatively you can contact
our Orderline on (0)1626 334555 or write to us
at FREEPOST EX2110, David & Charles Direct, Newton
Abbot, TQ12 4ZZ (no stamp required UK mainland).

Contents

Why the Bra?

The bra – necessary support, figure-enhancing frippery, object of seduction or device of torture? All of these, and more, depending on the bra, the wearer and the situation! Yet, whatever is said about the bra, one thing is clear: this diminutive undergarment has had an enormous impact on modern-day life. In shaping breasts, the bra has also shaped fashion and modern sex appeal. So for good or bad, it's time we acknowledge just what the bra means to each of us.

AA *Introduction*

The bra: a brief history

Breasts are a defining attribute of all that is female: timeless icons representing female sexuality and motherhood throughout history. Serving both function and fantasy, the bra is perhaps the most powerful element of a woman's wardrobe. What other item of clothing inspires such devotion, yearning, admiration, frustration and delight?

The bra has been around in one form or another for centuries. In fact, throughout history, women have used various contraptions to support and shape their breasts.

The early bras

The Cretans of 2500 BC favoured an open-cup device that lifted bare breasts up and out of their clothing, while active women of ancient Greece wore a binding called a *mastodeton* or *apodesmos* while exercising. Through the Middle Ages, women relied on long strips of fabric, which they would sling under a breast and around the shoulder. Divorce corsets were

worn in the late 18th century to lift and separate breasts, and as early as 1859 there were metallic bra-like constructions to hold matters rigidly in place.

However, bras as we know them today didn't appear until the late 19th century as a new, healthier feminine ideal was forming, one that included both athletic activity and employment outside the home. Despite the shift in mores, however, it wasn't until the invention of elastic in the early 20th century that bra manufacture and use became widespread.

BEFORE THE BRA
A progression of fabric bindings led up to the introduction of the corset in the15th century.

A CENTURY OF SUPPORT

1900–1919
War is finally declared on the corset and new forms of bust support appear. Corsets are no longer practical and the bra's

1920–1939
Thanks to suffragettes, women enjoy more freedom than ever before. The 1920s flapper girls demand flat chests but by the end of the 1930s pointy breasts are

1940–1959
The thrifty WWII years give way to a more glamorous era. Inspired by big-breasted Hollywood icons, women fit themselves into cone-shaped bras

The 20th century bra

While material use has played an enormous role in the types of bras worn, fashion has perhaps been a larger influence. Many of the first bras manufactured flattened breasts according to the youthful, boyish figures favoured by 'flappers'. By the mid-1930s, breasts became perky and unmissable, exemplified by Sweater Girl pin-ups and created by a new wave of bras that were designed to lift and separate. The trend towards high, unmoving breasts intensified in the 1940s, giving birth to the aggressively shaped 'bullet bust' made popular by Jane Russell in the movie *The Outlaw*. By the 1950s, the favoured female form was softer, rounder – à la Marilyn Monroe – and breasts became curvier and more pendulous.

Shape shifters

In the mid-1960s, models such as Twiggy and Jean Shrimpton made small, pert breasts fashionable again. This, combined with the burgeoning 'hippie' movement, led to a swing towards naturally shaped, unfettered breasts in the late 1960s and 1970s. Just a few years later, however, the athletic curves of late 1980s supermodels like Cindy Crawford sparked a demand for padded bras. The century moved to a close with the waifish figures of 1990 models like Kate Moss and Shalom Harlow, whose delicate bustlines spawned a renewed interest in natural-fitting, featherweight bras.

Up to date

By the millennium, the fashion pendulum had swung back to big. Large and globe-like are the breasts *du jour* and push-up bras, such as Wonderbra and Miracle Bra, created options for women wanting to pump-up their natural attributes. T-shirt and seamless bras are also widely available, suggesting we are now in the happy situation of anything goes!

> *"To the woman who thinks 'I Don't Need a Bra!' Pardon us, but you do."*

ADVERTISEMENT FOR MODEL BRASSIERE COMPANY 1917

1960–1979
What goes up must come down: the bra market hits the skids as waifs, hippies and women's lib all combine to hit bra sales hard. Softer

HELLO BOYS.

1980–1999
The lingerie business bounces back with lavish underwear and a new range of sports bras, while Madonna and the Wonderbra

2000+
The new millennium moves bras forward yet again. Now available to suit every figure, function and desire, the bra industry is bigger and better than ever.

In the starring role

Female breasts. They are a bra's *raison d'être*, with a fabulous variation in sizes, most weighing between two and 17 ounces. But it's what a breast can do that matters. Indeed, these appendages receive such attention for their sex appeal that it's easy to forget their original function is purely practical – to create the milk that nourishes newborn humans.

Notting Hill

Julia Roberts: What is it about men and nudity, particularly breasts? How can you be so interested in them?
Hugh Grant: Well...
Julia Roberts: Seriously, they're just breasts; every second person in the world has them.
Hugh Grant: More than that actually, when you think about it. Meatloaf has a very nice pair.
Julia Roberts: They're odd looking; they're for milk; your mother has them; you've seen a thousand of them. What's all the fuss about?
Hugh Grant: Actually, I can't think what it is really. Let me just have a quick look. (Hugh looks at Julia's naked bosoms.) No, no. Beats me!

BREAST FASCINATION
Best not to think too hard about why we love breasts so much –

What's all the fuss about?

Even so, there's no denying how many people get hot and bothered about what are essentially baby feeders. But why? What's behind breasts' sexy side? Theories abound. Some feel breast obsession is a sign of too-early weaning, or, the inevitable side-effect of a culture that was raised on baby formula. Others say our fixation shows a lack of maturity, a fear of adulthood. Still others say breasts represent a culture's feminine side, meaning the way a culture views breasts mirrors the way a culture sees and treats its female members.

Simply a thing of beauty

Desmond Morris argues – and pretty convincingly – that our breasts evolved to look like our buttocks, which were the body's primary sex signal before we stood on two feet. He points out that virtually all the sexual signals and erogenous zones are on the front of the body: the facial expressions, the lips, the breasts, the nipples, the genitals and the major blushing areas. Hmmm....maybe it's best not to think too hard about why we love breasts so much and just enjoy the beauty Mother Nature has so generously bestowed.

Bottoms up

In the seminal 1960s work *The Naked Ape*, Desmond Morris argued that buttocks were probably early human's primary sexual signal, attracting attention to the genitals and advertising rear access in our pre-bipedal days. According to Morris, once we started standing, our breasts evolved to mimic our buttocks.

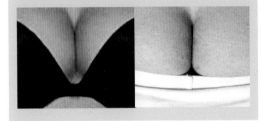

EYE CANDY
Despite their main role being to feed babies, our fascination with breasts knows no bounds. Big or small, women are as obsessed with enhancing them as men are at looking at them. In fact, whichever way we turn, there is sure to be a pair of buxom boobs gazing right back.

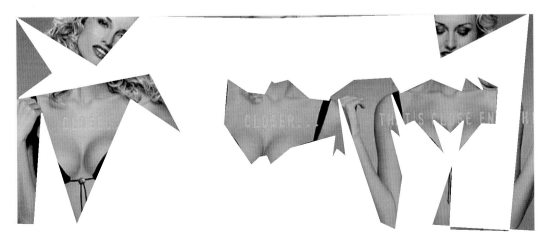

Function or frivolity?

Bras are practical, yes. We use them to keep our breasts in place, or to shunt them around to suit the latest fashion. Bras can be enhancing, too, padding our assets, disguising an overly generous bust, or giving tired breasts a perkier profile. Above all, the bra is a tool of seduction: a bra's lace or a strategically stray strap entice the viewer and make the wearer feel pretty damn sexy.

The average woman owns from four to ten bras, though she may only wear two or three of these with any regularity. Yet many fashion experts go as far as suggesting an entire bra wardrobe in a range of styles, ensuring you are equipped for every occasion. Even your everyday bra should be pretty (and clean!). Be honest, are you *still* wearing that grotty grey number you had on last night? Get rid!

EVERYDAY BRA
The key word for everyday bras is definitely 'comfort'.

Everyday bras

Consider what you like in an everyday bra – something seamless to slip unnoticed under your fitted T-shirts? Something to play up your delicate assets? Make a list of what you like and need in your everyday bra and search until you find a comfortable model that meets those needs. Once you've found it, get

PROTECTING YOUR MODESTY
Do we really need bras? Probably not. There's no medical reason to wear one. But they do hold matters beautifully in place until you are ready to reveal yourself as nature intended.

yourself at least three of them. This will ensure that you always have a clean one ready. When that gorgeous guy hits you like a truck on an impromptu night out, you don't want to spoil the spontaneity just because you're wearing Bridget Jones pants and a mismatched manky bra. Or, when that gormless guy hits you *with* a truck, you know you don't really want that dreamboat doctor to cut away your designer clothes only to reveal grimy, grey skivvies underneath. Of course, what's under your undies has got to look good too. Add a sports bra to your shopping list. It will help reduce exercise-induced sagging and embarrassing bounce.

"I do wish my breasts were bigger. Not big... but less small."

CALISTA FLOCKHART

BABS' BOOBS
Avoid any embarrassing incidents (remember Barbara Windsor, left, about to lose her bra in *Carry on Camping?*), by making sure your bra is up to the task at hand.

Eveningwear
A backless or strapless style may be necessary under formal attire. A convertible bra can be helpful if you wear a large variety of necklines, backless outfits and sleeveless shirts. As its name suggests, a convertible bra has adjustable straps that allow the bra to be transformed into a halter, racerback, one-shoulder or strapless style. A long-line bra is an old-fashioned looking

SIMPLY DIVINE
Off for breakfast at Tiffany's again? The look just

THE BIG DAY
For obvious reasons, wedding lingerie is almost as important as the dress itself. Make sure your bra doesn't get any unnecessary exposure though, and wear

EARLY EROTICA
Saucy underwear is certainly not a new concept, as this 1920s French postcard demonstrates. Sexy or what?

"I just accept them as a great accessory to every outfit."

JENNIFER LOVE HEWITT, ON HER BREASTS

CHEATING NATURE
If you feel you've been hard done by on the cleavage front, a padded push-up bra will make your breasts appear

thing, midriff-skimming in length and with waist panels to help slim the figure. Despite its dated appearance, the long-line bra remains popular for the smooth, sleek silhouette it imparts. Racerback bras feature the same T-back or X-back as many competition-style swimsuits. The advantage of this back style is twofold: not only do the centre-anchored straps render the bra invisible under similarly styled shirts, they are terrific for narrow-shouldered women who have difficulty keeping traditional bra straps on the shoulders.

Bras for seduction

A demi-cup bra is a must-have for seduction – and a flattering choice for small to medium breasts. The contoured, underwired cups are partially cut away in order to expose the top of the breast. The shoulder straps are usually set on the wide side, allowing you to wear a large variety of low necklines. A push-up bra can be used to give extra lift to breasts of any size. Again, it is particularly helpful in giving small and medium breasts a fuller look but push-up bras are available to give already ample boobs an extra boost. Push-up bras have extra padding at the underside of each cup, and incorporate a variety of ingenious gadgets to push breasts high up on the chest.

TO THE EXTREME
This cleavage-enhancing bra has removable foam pads, giving maximum cleavage for ultimate seduction.

Double-troubleshooting tips

It is estimated that 60 to 80 per cent of women do not know their correct bra measurements! Breasts change size with time, which is why bra-fitting experts recommend re-evaluating your measurements at least once every two years. See the appendix (at the back of the book) for tips on fitting your bra. However, having your bra fitted professionally is still the best option.

Back-band rides up: Fasten the hook on a tighter enclosure, go down one band size, or loosen your bra's shoulder straps.
Loose or wrinkled cups: Go down one cup size.
Breasts spill out of cups: Try a larger cup size or choose a bra style that offers more coverage through the cups.
Red strap marks: Loosen the bra's straps, place padding underneath them or try a more breast-supportive bra.
Falling straps: Tighten the straps or try a different style of bra, such as a T-back, U-back or racerback style.
One breast bigger than the other: Don't worry, all women are a bit asymmetrical. Fit the cup to the larger breast, then tighten the strap a bit on the smaller side. If necessary, you can have your bras custom-made.

Before the Bra

In this chapter we delve into the bras of bygone days. And, yes, although there weren't any 'brassieres' as such, there were breast bindings and bandeaux (some of which were similar to sports bras of today). But it was the corset, popularized by Catherine de Medici in the mid-16th century, and not the bra, which reigned supreme from Renaissance times until the early 20th century. Stiff, heavy, tight, and often fashioned with whalebone or steel rods, corsets were uncomfortable, and so restrictive they damaged women's health. Roll on the bra!

A *Pre-1900*

Before the corset

What did women do with their breasts before the corset was introduced? Alas, historians have paid relatively scant attention to the subject, but evidence of ancient bra-like clothing has been found all over the globe.

DRESS LIKE AN EGYPTIAN
A statue of the mythical nymph Daphne, wearing a form of Egyptian bust support, 5th or 6th century AD.

The first breast supports

- 3500 BC During the Bronze Age, early Germanic tribes tied bands of cloth or animal skins around their chests while working in order to keep breasts comfortably in place.
- 3000+ BC Naked female breasts were a common sight in ancient Egypt. The most support breasts got was in the form of a *kalasiris*, a simple tube of cloth that was typically worn at the waist and held by two 'suspenders' of fabric that laid against the breasts.
- 2500 BC The women of Crete worshipped a bare-breasted 'Snake Goddess'. Statues found on the Greek island indicate Cretan women wore an early bra-corset device. This garment, which was fitted from under the breasts to the waist, aggressively emphasized the breasts in honour of the goddess. Called a *mastoeides*, the breast supporter served to push the breasts up and out of the wearer's clothing. A bit like an uber push-bra. To further emphasize their bare, very perky breasts, Minoan misses donned short, bolero-type jackets that were cut away in front to show off the bust.
- 1500 BC In Vedic times, the breast-band was used as support by Indian women. Over this, they wore a *cholika*, which was

originally a square piece of cloth with a slit for the neck. The *cholika* developed into a more bra-like garment with the addition of string that was attached to make it backless and fold beneath the breasts. Royal ladies wore decorated *cholika* made from elegant, diaphanous material.
- 1000 BC Female Mongolian warriors bound their breasts with criss-crossing fabric strips.
- 360 AD Women in France wore a band of cloth called a *bandeau* across their breasts.
- 1200 AD In Circassia, an area on the Black Sea north of Caucasus Mountain, girls were tightly bound in elaborate but painful corsets designed to keep their breasts, ribcages and waists from growing. These corsets, which ran from collar to waist, were worn during bathing and even sleeping, and featured two wooden planks across the chest held by leather binding.

MINOAN STYLE
Women in Bronze Age Crete wore a push-up corset with a cutaway jacket so that their bare breasts were lifted out of their clothes and exposed.

PLAYING GAMES
Roman women in the 3rd and 4th centuries wore a Greek-inspired band of material around their breasts, not only to reduce movement whilst taking part in games, but also to conceal the development of a mature bust.

Medieval misery

During the 13th to 15th centuries, there was not a bra to be had, meaning most women left their breasts free. However, the arrival of tailors in the late 1200s resulted in more shapely garments, which needed laced-up bodices.

Early medieval fashions looked dreary at best: long, shapeless tunics and smocks. Colours were dull browns and greens, and wool was the textile of choice (not that there *was* any choice!).

Bust bodices

If you happened to be a wealthy nobleperson, however, the 13th century was much more fashionable. Tailors (finally!) learnt techniques to make more shapely garments, creating a demand for laced-up bodices. Women began showing off their waists and flattening their breasts with short, trim bodices that were worn over a cloth blouse and above a full skirt. However, these bodices weren't underwear, they were, indeed, corsets – worn on the outside!

Calamitous century

The silhouette at the start of the 14th century was flat, flat, flat. There was little around to raise the spirits, let alone the breasts: the crusades were still hogging the headlines; the hundred years war between France and England seemed to be going on for, well, a hundred years; and peasants were revolting all over the place. Oh, and a plague had claimed the lives of over a third of the population of Europe. With all this misery, breasts somehow lost their importance. And, anyway, the omnipotent Catholic Church made it plain that it found the clear outline of a woman's curves indecent. Consequently, fashion featured design devices that pulled the gaze away from breasts, such as long, tubular bodices, wide full skirts and high ruffled collars.

Renaissance eroticism

As the 14th century drew to a close, and the medieval period gave way to the Renaissance, the bodice's neckline crept lower and things started to liven up.

FASHION RENAISSANCE
Fashions of the 1400s saw lower, off-the-shoulder necklines, leading wealthier women to wear corsets for the first time.

MORE VARIETY AND STYLE
As tailors became more skilled, women were able to reject the shapeless smocks of earlier years and show off their waists and shape their figures.

AGNES SOREL

Among the eroticized breasts of the Renaissance, the most celebrated of all were those of Agnes Sorel, mistress of France's King Charles VII. Round, high and compact, her glorious globes were considered the aesthetic ideal by fashion followers of the time.

In the 15th century, the Renaissance, characterized by a renewed appreciation of beauty, moved into full swing. Breasts began to be eroticized – not just any breasts, but the compact, rounded breasts of the upper classes (the lower classes, who breastfed their own and the upper classes' children, had decidedly less perky breasts).

Necklines dipped so low that the tops – sometimes even the nipples – of breasts were exposed. In some aristocratic circles, the whole breast was exposed, and sat on a shelf created by the top of a woman's bodice.

While a bodice did a fine job of moulding breasts, many wealthy women donned a garment that hadn't been widely worn before – the corset! These breast-to-waist garments were made of muslin or linen that had been stiffened with a gluey paste and employed lacing to tighten or loosen them. The Age of the Corset was just around the corner...

> *"No woman will support the bust by the disposition of a blouse or by tightened dress."*
>
> EDICT OF STRASBOURG 1370

The corset years

Corsets paved the way for bras, but in the 16th, 17th and 18th centuries they were essential to the day's attire. How else could a woman achieve the shifting costume shapes of the era?

Corsets were the precursors to modern-day bras. After all, corsets trained not only women's breasts, but their eyes, encouraging them to see a moulded breast as normal. Indeed, corsets trained society's eyes, making lifted, shaped breasts an expected part of the female silhouette.

WAIST NOT, WANT NOT
The upper classes led the way during the rise of the corset, but not everyone was happy about the shrinking waist lines.

The 16th century

The 1500s were an exciting time for clothing. Couture watchers call the period a time of transition, an era of sumptuous fabrics and dramatic silhouettes following centuries of dull, often shapeless, garb. It was a time to show off! There were newly minted middle and merchant classes, as well as tailoring innovations, exciting textile discoveries, and an adventurous spirit wafting through Europe. The frocks of the 15th century were now replaced by a separate skirt and lace-fastened bodice. Fashionable bodices became more elongated and tighter, with increasingly flatter bustlines. Women had to turn to undergarments to help them squeeze into their bodices, to compress their breasts and to give their torsos a smooth line. Hence, the under-bodice, or corset. These under-bodices were

A TIME OF TRANSITION
Lace-fastened bodices replaced the simpler frocks of the 15th century, forcing women to turn to corsets in an attempt to squeeze into them.

made from paste-stiffened linen and given support by thin wooden planks called busks. (Some of these were so ornate that it became popular to wear clothing that revealed the gorgeous underwear beneath.) Iron or steel was soon added to reinforce the under-bodice, and by the 1530s, iron corsets were being worn by the upper classes.

Catherine de Medici

Every era has at least one iconic fashion figure. When it comes to the corset, that person was Catherine de Medici. When Catherine married the soon-to-be French king, Henry II, she enjoyed a commanding presence and was to bring in her famous edict banning 'thick waists' at court. Soon a naturally proportioned waist became a vulgar sign of the lower classes, something no upwardly mobile lady wanted.

The fashion migrated to other countries and soon the women of Elizabethan England and the rest of Europe were compressing themselves with restrictive corsets to achieve the 13-inch waist and small breasts that the young queen favoured. Ironically, even a corset couldn't help Catherine's waist remain small or her breasts compact.

The 17th century

As the 16th century rolled to an end, women were squeezing themselves into corsets, trying to achieve a tubular torso with flat, high breasts. And so it continued into the new century, allowing common people's wardrobes to catch up with those of the moneyed classes. It was during the 1600s that corset-wearing began to trickle down to the working classes, who wore cast-off corsets from richer folk or fashioned their own. These homemade garments were typically stiffened with easy-to-find materials such as reeds, wood strips or paste.

As the busk grew in popularity, the fashionable torso became tighter and tighter, until women began tightlacing their corsets to achieve an extra narrow ribcage and waist. Something had to give, and breasts were finally given more room – and more freedom! – as the century progressed.

CATHERINE DE MEDICI
Paintings of the queen show that after childbearing, the middle-aged lady had become somewhat portly. Thus, in her last years, Catherine concerned herself with politics, leaving fashion to others.

> "It made the wearers look as if they were imprisoned in a closely fitting fortress."
>
> A CONTEMPORARY WRITER ON THE CATHERINE DE MEDICI-STYLE CORSET

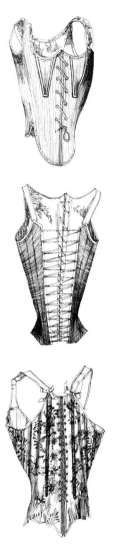

TAILOR-MADE
Ornate busks were often inserted into the front of corsets, pushing the breasts high up on the ribcage.

18TH CENTURY BODICES
Although these different styles of bodice show great attention to detail, it is not hard to imagine the torture caused by them!

In the 17th century, breasts were completely – or nearly – exposed by low necklines. Other fashion changes included lighter, softer corsets – no more metal stays or iron corsets – stiffened with whalebone, paste or reeds.

The 18th century

The 1700s were a confusing time when it came to breast fashions. At the beginning of the period, breasts were doing the same thing they were doing during the late 1600s – sitting high on the chest, pressed against the ribcage by a torso-tightening corset. And that's where they stayed until the middle of the century, when breasts crept downwards a bit! Yes, they were still moulded into a gentle swell instead of separated and held as two exaggerated orbs. But their tops – what the ancient Greeks called 'breast buttocks' – often showed above the plunging necklines of court gowns. Depending on a woman's comfort, and the particular court, some nipple might protrude. To support these bared beauties, corsets were lowered in front.

Breasts got a makeover near the 1780s, when many women embraced the column dress, modelled after the

BREAST EXPOSURE
Breasts may have finally headed south during the 1600s but necklines dropped even lower, often exposing a large amount of heaving bosom, and sometimes the occasional nipple.

'country dresses' worn by English gentry (think *Pride and Prejudice*). Historians reckon this style, which was adopted by the French after the revolution, was a direct reaction against the excess of the French aristocracy. So, almost overnight, trendsetters like Josephine (and other ladies of Europe's courts) shed their hooped skirts and corsets, and donned simple, lightweight frocks with 'empire' waistlines that sat directly below the bustline. That's right, for the first time in centuries, women weren't wearing corsets! Imagine how strange that would have been for a woman, after decades of binding, to go without her stays! Instead, most women wore a camisole-like undershirt that offered some support without shaping or binding the breasts, ribs or waist. Breasts were still shaped into a monobosom, but this time, the uni-breast rested, shelf-like, above the dress's waistband. No more shoving or flattening!

Orthopaedic corset

With such extreme fashion standards to be met, desperate women would go to great measures to achieve the tiny waistlines that were demanded of them. As the bottom five ribs are not attached to the sternum, gradually tightening a corset would eventually push them up and in, creating a smaller girth. It is even rumoured that some women were so desperate to achieve a tiny midriff that they had some of their ribs removed. Corsets were not only used to squeeze a woman's waist into wasp-like proportions, however; this frightening-looking 19th century device was actually invented to correct deformities of the bones or muscles.

Age of the hourglass

The 1800s could be summed up as all cinched waists and hourglass shapes. Sadly, the fashion of tightlacing condemned women to not only discomfort but health dangers.

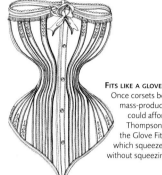

FITS LIKE A GLOVE
Once corsets became mass-produced everyone could afford one. Thompsons created the Glove Fitting Corset, which squeezed the waist without squeezing the wallet.

If you've been reading along, you know that the 18th century ended with the column dress, an empire-waisted frock that was worn sans-corset. Unfortunately, this trend lasted only a short while. Women were too accustomed to wearing some kind of bust support to give it up, and society was too used to seeing women's bust safeguarded by something. But what?

By 1820, the corset was the only existing option, so women returned to it. In response, waists became cinched-thin, bosoms were lifted, stiff and without a hint of movement, and hips were padded and encased in petticoat-supported skirts so full that women couldn't navigate through crowds. In short, fashion was moving toward the hourglass.

The hourglass figure

To create the extreme hourglass shape that would attract admiring male attention, young women began cinching their laces tightly. Earlier corsets laced up the back, which was fine considering the aristocratic ladies who wore them had maids to help. The 19th century models typically laced up the front, allowing women of all stations to wear them. Furthermore, improved methods of manufacture, and particularly the invention of the sewing-machine, made mass-produced corsets affordable to everyone, including

IT'S A CINCH
Women went to extreme lengths to achieve the fashionable hourglass figure of the 1800s, which demanded a waist measuring no more than 21 inches.

STRAIGHT-LACED
The corset was designed to shape the figure, but it also had a moral function, directing its wearer to exercise self-restraint and act in a ladyike manner. A female of 'lax morals', and lacking the correct undergarments, was known as a 'loose woman'.

Over the shoulder

In the late 19th century, French corset-maker Herminie Cadolle invented the bra-like *Bien-Être* ('well-being') bust supporter. Unlike traditional corsets, which squeezed breasts up, the *Bien-Être* bodice supported them using shoulder straps. While the device was marketed in France as a health aid, it escaped widespread notice.

working and rural classes. Soon, regardless of class, a fashionable miss had a waist which measured 21 inches or less. 'Your waist should be no bigger around than your age,' claimed a popular 19th century maxim. Tightlacing continued for the next hundred years, as corsets became longer and tighter through the mid-1800s, flattening down the breasts before pushing them back up with the S-bend corset in the 1890s. However, one thing remained constant – the wasp-like waist. Women really did suffer for fashion.

The price of tightlacing

Magazines advocated lacing up young girls to ensure their feminine behaviour. Whether it made a woman behave more demurely is debatable, but it did create a large population of adult females with deformed

Prototype bra

Back in the US, in 1893, Marie Tucek patented the 'Breast Supporter'. The garment included both separate supportive cups for each breast and shoulder straps that passed over the shoulders and fastened with hook and eye closures. It was remarkably similar to the demi-cup bras we are wearing today, which makes it one of the earliest prototype bras. The device was worn by a few of Tucek's friends, but wasn't widely accepted in the corset-wearing culture of the late 19th century. In her patent text, she referred to the separate cups as 'pockets'.

ribcages and misplaced internal organs. Unable to expand their lungs enough to draw sufficient oxygen, women regularly fainted. Internal organs were lacerated by broken ribs. To flatten the protruding belly caused by all these out-of-place organs, women wore the spoon busk, an industrial-strength stiffened panel that sat against the stomach.

Women miscarried. Corset-wearing mothers were unable to breast feed. Women died. And, still, tightlacing continued. A few enlightened folk protested against tightlacing. Called reformers, these women and men were often linked with the early feminist movement, others were physicians, religious types or everyday folk who were repulsed by the bound waist, immovable bust and impossibly full skirts of the day.

Unfortunately for women, corsets wouldn't be completely rejected until early in the next century, when the bra made its very welcome appearance on the undergarment scene. In the 21st century, corsets have found a niche in the erotica market.

DEAD FASHIONABLE
This 19th century French diagram shows the damage women were doing to their internal organs by wearing such tight-fitting corsets. Organs were misplaced and lung capacity reduced, causing fainting and even death.

CREATING CORSETS
As a fashionable figure was required at all times, it was necessary to have a corset for every occasion. This meant big business across the globe and during the 1890s, 433 corset designs were trademarked in France alone.

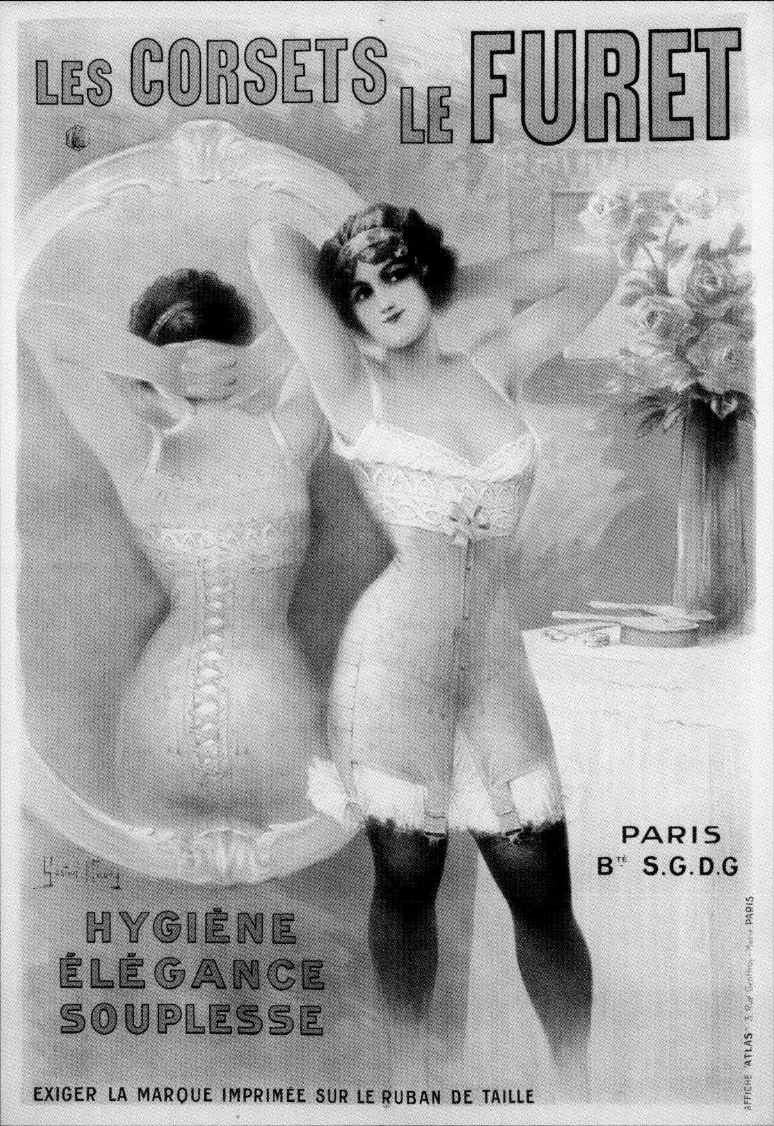

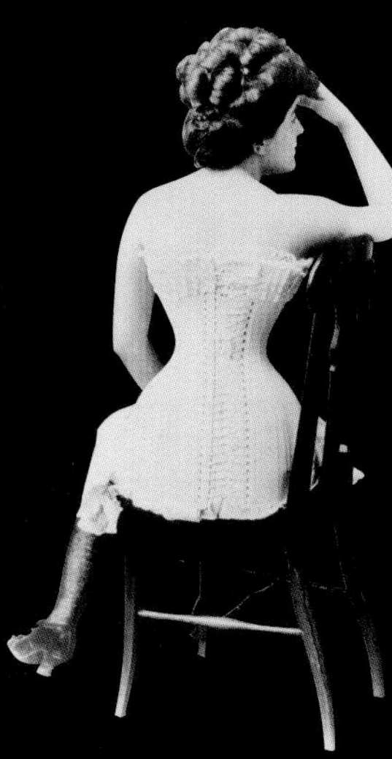

LES CORSETS LE FURET
PARIS
Bté S.G.D.G
HYGIÈNE
ÉLÉGANCE
SOUPLESSE
EXIGER LA MARQUE IMPRIMÉE SUR LE RUBAN DE TAILLE
AFFICHE "ATLAS" 3, Rue Geoffroy-Marie, PARIS

TIME FOR A CHANGE
By the end of the 19th century, women had had it with the corset. Uncomfortable, dangerous, stuffy and old-fashioned-looking, it was time to release the waist and start concentrating on the bust.

$150
18F 219

$150
18F 264

$150
18F 268

98¢
18F127

48¢

$1.35
18F132

The Bra Wars

At the dawn of the 20th century, the world began to look more like it does today: cars appeared on city streets and electricity came into use. Fashion, too, took on a recognizable silhouette. Women still wore corsets, but dresses were growing shorter and more casual. And so was the underwear! This was the start of the bra era; the corset was on the way out, slowly but surely. After all, how could women resist the bra's allure? As sexy as a corset, but a whole lot easier to wear.

B *1900–1919*

> *"I can't say the brassiere will ever take as great a place in history as the steamboat, but I did invent it."*
>
> MARY PHELPS JACOB

Mary Phelps Jacob

So who did actually invent the bra? Well, Phelps Jacob claims she did. In 1913, she purchased a glamorous, sheer evening gown for a party. Unfortunately, her corset not only left strange bumps below her party frock, it was also easily seen beneath the diaphanous fabric. To solve this problem she took two silk handkerchiefs, some pink ribbon and thread, and fashioned a breast-supporting device that was not only pretty and comfortable, but also practically invisible under her gown. This 'invisible undergarment' caused quite a stir and she spent most of 1913 duplicating her 'backless brassiere' for interested friends. She applied for a US patent, which was awarded on 3 November 1914, making Mary Phelps Jacob the first person to patent a device called a brassiere.

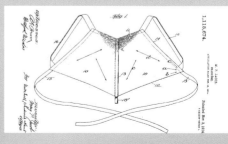

A bra is born

1904

Successful corset-maker Charles De Bevoise invents a lightweight undergarment fashioned in silk and embroidered with lace. He calls it the 'brassiere'.

The De Bevoise Company was in the business of creating good-looking underwear for ladies. In the late 1800s, these underthings were corsets and the like, but as the 20th century neared, fashion began changing and women began demanding something more comfortable than the corset. Clearly, the bra was the modern answer to women's breast-holding – and breast-moulding – needs.

Silk and lace

De Bevoise's main innovation was the use of dainty fabrics such as silk or sheer cotton embroidered with lace. Between 1904 and 1920, the De Bevoise Company offered over 20 different brassiere styles, most available in a range of fabric, colour and trimming choices.

However, these early brassieres still flattened breasts, rather than cradling them in separate cups or lifting them from the shoulders. In fact, they were more like modern camisoles than bras as we know them today, creating an unyielding, cleavage-less monobosom.

NOT SO NATURAL
Corset adverts claimed that they followed the 'natural form', but women wanted more comfort.

A booming trade

So although we have Charles to thank for naming the bra, it was certainly not his invention. Nor, of course, was he alone in his innovative endeavours. Among those creating brassieres were Alfred Benjamin, Rose Kleinert, Laura Blanche Lyon, Madeleine Gabeau, Gabrielle Poix and Samuel Gossard. Some of these contraptions were short corsets, others tight, pull-on, half-camisoles. Some had separate cups. Some pulled over the head. Others fastened in front, back or at the side. All helped push bra research and development forward.

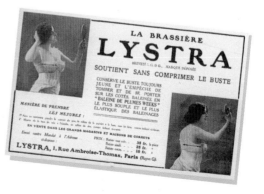

PARTY ON
Despite controversy surrounding its inventor, the birth of the bra was a monumental occasion from which women never looked back.

A NEW TYPE OF LIFT
New brassieres offered support without squashing the bust. This French bra used whalebone as an early form of underwire.

The new wave

1908

Paris fashion designer Paul Poiret declares war on the corset, and openly encourages the use of the brassiere by designing a new range of classically inspired, streamlined dresses.

Although Poiret didn't claim to invent the bra per se, he did claim to abolish its rival, the corset. He did this by designing elegant, comfortable, streamlined clothing – a fashion first – that was worn without traditional corsets. In his own words, he 'liberated the breasts'. *Vive la France!*

A one-man crusade

Poiret was a larger-than-life character and the first fashion celebrity. His personal crusade against the corset began in 1904 when, after training at the House of Worth and Doucet, he set up on his own and designed his 'Nouvelle Vague' line, featuring gowns that did not require corsets underneath them. He was inspired by classical dress that celebrated the natural female form; he abhorred the 'rotten gadgets' that gave women such unnatural outlines. He invited high-society clientele to visit his salon to see his outrageous gowns paraded by beautiful models.

GOING TO NEW LENGTHS
Classically inspired elegant dresses, such as 'Le Pouf', 1929, were designed to enhance rather than restrict the female form.

FREE THE BREAST!
Poiret famously declared: 'It was in the name of Liberty that I advocated against the corset and in favour of the brassiere.'

STREAMLINED DESIGNS
Poiret railed against the S-bend corset,
complaining that they made women look
as if they were 'hauling a trailer'.

MADAME POIRET
Married to Paul Poiret in 1905,
Denise regularly modelled her
husband's designs, which included
a pair of scandalous harem
pantaloons at the launch party for
the '1002 Nights' range in 1911.

*"It was the era of
the corset. I declared
war on it!"*

PAUL POIRET

These included his wife Denise. His gowns caused great excitement among his clients. When the Countess Greffulhe, uncontested queen of the salons in Faubourg Saint-Germain, Paris, wore one of his scandalous 'sheaths' to her daughter's wedding, his success was assured.

Designer to the stars

In 1908, Poiret set out his design manifesto in an illustrated brochure entitled 'Les Robes de Paul Poiret'. He quickly became the designer to the stars and dressed the likes of Ida Rubinstein, Isadora Duncan, Eleanore Duse and Sarah Bernhardt. Poiret also hobnobbed with many of the foremost artists of his day, including Georges Lepape and Raoul Dufy. Dufy designed bold textile prints for Poiret's elegant dresses, cloaks and shawls.

Give them what they want?

In 1909, Poiret became fascinated by harem girls and designed shocking outfits based on harem pants in shimmering colours with beaded embellishments. He created kimonos, turbans and aigrettes inspired by Diaghilev's exotic *Ballets Russes,* which provoked a huge amount of interest in Europe. In 1911, the self-professed 'liberator' introduced his notorious hobble skirt, worn with a 'fetter' that restricted the wearer to tiny steps in imitation of Japanese geisha girls. He may have freed the breasts and the waist, but he shackled the legs!

Despite Poiret's gallant efforts, we will see later that it took a world war to effectively see off the corset. Unfortunately, the war saw off Poiret too. He closed shop to join the military in 1914 and he was never again able to provide clothes to suit post-war women. Other designers, such as Lanvin, stepped into his bejewelled oriental slippers. And it was left to Coco Chanel to really hand women their sartorial freedom.

THE HOBBLE SKIRT
Despite his quest to liberate women's breasts, Poiret created a new nuisance for women in 1911 by launching the infamous hobble skirt. It allowed women to take only tiny, tottering steps and made climbing into cars extremely difficult.

THE BRASSIERE IN VOGUE
The Model Brassiere Company designed underwear that complemented the elegant dresses of the time and allowed women to move freely.

FACTORY FASHION
During WWI, millions of women filled positions left vacant by the men who joined the forces. Some women left jobs in the domestic service industry to work gruelling hours in grimy munitions factories.

The patriotic bustline

1914

The outbreak of World War I deals a mortal blow to the corset and increases the popularity of the bra, ensuring the garment a lasting place in women's undie drawers.

The rigours of the Great War and the shortages that inevitably followed in its wake meant everyone had to make sacrifices. It was considered vulgar to wear jewellery and lavish clothes, women wore their hair shorter and dresses, too, became shorter due to a shortage of fabric. Women from the upper classes took on voluntary philanthropic work, which broadened their horizons and put them into direct contact with 'the great unwashed', many of them enrolling in the Red Cross as nurses. There was an intermingling of classes that was hitherto unthinkable.

Women at work

When war broke out and practically all able-bodied men had been conscripted into the armed forces, the women went to work, taking over the traditionally male roles to keep their country going. For the first time, women were working in factories making munitions, taking administrative roles in offices, driving trams, delivering post and lighting lamps. Underwear at this time needed to allow easy movement and be comfortable enough to wear during a long working day. Lightweight materials that were soft against the skin

A SHINING EXAMPLE
Florence Nightingale had banned her nurses from wearing corsets, as they made it difficult to perform even the simplest task. Red Cross volunteers in WWI followed her example.

replaced the heavy corset-weight fabric used by early bra makers.

Constricting corsets were completely impractical. They became shorter and more pliable and were gradually replaced by the girdle. But if girdles were used for slimming the waist and hips, what was to be done with the breasts? En masse, women finally took notice of the bra. It had been around in one form or another for decades, but now it became indispensable.

Hard times

Many bra manufacturers, however, were struggling to survive the rigours of war and the inevitable shortage of raw materials, and many businesses failed. Those that survived streamlined their production systems and simplified their designs, which was to stand them in good stead for when the war ended.

The market for their product was to grow dramatically in the post-war period. After making do and mending during the war years (bras were often improvised from handkerchiefs and other scraps of material), more and more women were ready to enjoy the convenience of ready-made, off-the-shelf bras.

Women in uniform

Although women did join the military during WWI, the roles they carried out were still largely traditional 'women's work': cooking, cleaning and clerical, and some driving. (It was during WWII that women first worked as mechanics and fired anti-aircraft guns.) Women doing men's work was very much a temporary arrangement. Female personnel wore uniforms modelled on those of their male comrades, with simple lines and solemn colours (coloured dyes were prohibitively expensive). This male-influenced clothing infused fashion with a spare, utilitarian ethos. To conserve valuable fabric, clothing was cut closer to the body, hems became shorter, and undergarments became much skimpier.

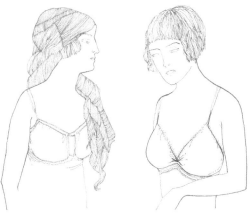

ONE BECOMES TWO
The earliest reference to bra cups was in two different US patents issued in 1916. Before this time, most brassieres had no separate areas for each breast. Those that did referred to these divisions as 'pockets' rather than cups.

Death blow to the corset

On 6 April 1917, despite strong protest from the American public, President Woodrow Wilson declared war on Germany. This was a major victory for the bra! The need to make vast quantities of munitions put metals in short supply. The US War Industries Board called on women to stop buying corsets, which, at the time, typically contained steel support. This freed up an eye-popping 28,000 tons of metal (enough to build two battleships!) and encouraged those few, full-corset wearing holdouts to try the bra.

A crisis of conscience

America had a crisis of conscience over the question of whether or not it should enter the war. And many American women, along with conscientious objectors from all nations, initially focused their efforts on winning the peace. The Women's Peace Party (WPP) grew out of the women's suffrage movement to address the causes of war and find a peaceful solution. In 1915, the WPP held an International Conference of Women (from both sides of the war) at the Hague, in the Netherlands, to call for mediation.

The Yanks are coming

Once America entered the war in 1917, over 25,000 American women headed for Europe. As well as helping to nurse the wounded, they helped provide food and other supplies to the military, served as telephone operators, or entertained the troops. Thirteen thousand American women enlisted in the US Navy, mostly performing clerical duties but, nonetheless, they were the first women in US history to be admitted to full military status. The army, too, hired female nurses and telephone operators to work overseas, but as civilian employees (despite the fact that they wore uniforms).

IF YOU WANT TO FIGHT!

Howard Chandler Christy. 1915.

JOIN THE MARINES

WAKE UP, AMERICA!

CIVILIZATION CALLS EVERY MAN WOMAN AND CHILD!
MAYOR'S COMMITTEE 50 EAST 42nd ST

THE SLEEPING GIANT
Public support was crucial to the US involvement in the war. The US government used posters to ask its people to 'wake up' and recognize the 'threat to civilization', calling upon *all* citizens to do their bit.

FIGHTING FOR FREEDOM
This WWI poster depicts a woman in full military garb with bayonet at the ready. In fact, women's work during WWI was largely confined to very mundane work such as cooking, cleaning and clerical work.

The spy with the golden bra

1917

Mata Hari, the 'courtesan' famed for her extravagant bras and many affairs with high-ranking military officers, is tried by a French military court and shot as a spy.

Mata Hari was an exotic dancer popular before and during World War I. She may or may not have also been a spy, but she was certainly an early bra enthusiast. Her life was fascinating, but ultimately very tragic.

A tragic beginning

Born Margaretha Zelle in Leeuwarden, Holland, Mata Hari was the daughter of a well-to-do Dutch milliner and his homemaker wife. Little Margaretha enjoyed a particularly pampered childhood. When she was 13, however, her father lost his fortune and deserted the family. Her mother went mad then died, leaving 15-year-old Margaretha and her four brothers parentless. After bouncing between relatives, Margaretha answered a personal ad from a Dutch naval officer seeking marriage. He responded and the two married in 1885. To cut a long story short, Margaretha's husband was a drunk, womanizing, raping, wife-beater. They divorced in 1900.

A new life in Paris

Left without funds or a way to support herself, Margaretha went to Paris and gave herself the Malay name Mata Hari (which means 'eye of the dawn') and tried on the life of an exotic dancer. There was only one problem – two problems actually – her breasts. They were very small, and Mata was self-conscious about baring them. The solution came from Paris's premier undergarment maker Codille: Mata would wear a nude-coloured body stocking – making her appear naked, but covering her pubic hair – topped with

a jewelled brassiere. The sparkling bra was never removed, and Mata stuffed it with cotton to exaggerate her assets.

Keeping Mata's in place

To say that Mata was a European sensation is putting it mildly. Men vied for her attention and Mata became a well-loved courtesan. Supported and pampered by her male admirers, she enjoyed a succession of lovers from Europe's various military forces. It was said that even during sex, Mata's bra stayed put. When asked to remove it, she refused, saying she'd been attacked by an animal, or some such horror story. In some circles at least, she soon became as famous for her gorgeous bras as she was for her dancing.

Spy bra

Whether or not Mata's bra was really padded with microfilm, we may never know. However, many 'technobras' have been developed over the years that double as radios or tape recorders, although it is hard to imagine how some of the designs might be concealed beneath a sexy negligee.

THE SPARKLING BRA

Exotic dancer and possible spy, Mata Hari loved her jewelled stage bra so much that it is rumoured she even kept it on during sex.

A TRAGIC END

Mata Hari was accused of espionage by the French, but wrongly accused, say most modern historians. Nevertheless, she was executed by firing squad on 15 October 1917. Mata refused a blindfold, blew a kiss to her executors, and was killed by a bullet to the heart.

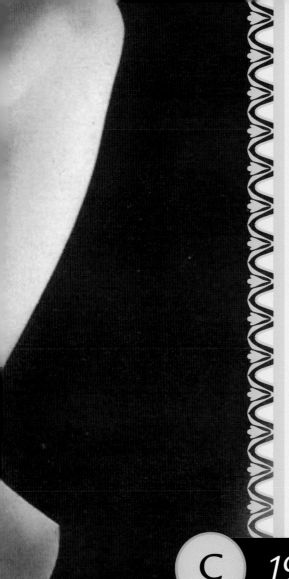

The Jazz Years

For women and their bras, this period was the most liberating of all. As they began to lead more active lives, women continued to discard their restricting corsets in favour of the bra. In the 1920s, the flapper girls created a vogue for bandeaux and minimizing bras but in the 1930s voluptuous breasts bounced back, with Hollywood stars promoting the new Sweater Girl look. Despite widespread deprivation in the early 1930s, sales of bras were strong, as women revelled in the freedom of their new underwear.

C *1920–1939*

Votes for women

1920

The 19th Amendment declared: 'The right of citizens of the United States to vote shall not be denied or abridged by the United States or by any State on account of sex.'

Two years earlier in Britain, after the suffragettes' long struggle, women had finally been given the vote. Women in Australia, New Zealand and most of Canada had also been granted voting rights. The US realized it was going to have to follow suit. Emancipation of women was finally a reality.

Freedom is near

Ironically, while women were finally achieving empowerment politically, they were still struggling to find a comfortable form of bust apparel! The suffragette movement was, in many ways, emulated by the concurrent history of the bra.

As the feminist movement burgeoned, the corset was seen as an unnecessary evil hampering female emancipation. And, quite simply, this was true. After all, there's a serious limit to what a person can achieve when she's not able to perform even the simple action of bending at the waist!

For these early feminists, the corset perpetuated the myth of the helpless female, prone to fainting fits and 'hysteria' at the slightest provocation. It was a situation that suited the archetypal Victorian patriarch to a tee. The corset served the same purpose in Western Europe and North America as the binding of feet did in China. It made a woman less physically capable and so more dependent on the men in her life, be they father, brother or husband.

DOING IT FOR THEMSELVES
The seeds of the 19th Amendment were sown as early as 1848, at the first North American Women's Rights Convention. These early suffragettes would have been corseted but by the 1920s things were improving – most women could vote and underwear was becoming more comfortable.

One of the boys

Although in later years the bra became labelled a symbol of female oppression, in the 1910s and 1920s it was a symbol of freedom, as we shall see shortly. The bra enabled women to run, play sports, dance and drive – just as men did. Women of today have a big debt of gratitude to the feminists of this era.

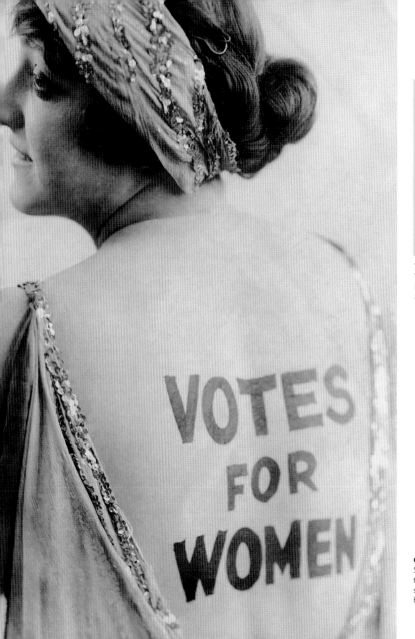

THE SEARCH FOR PERFECTION
Women were delighted at the
increasing availability – and
acceptability – of the bra.

*"Men
make the
moral code
and expect
women to
accept it."*

EMMELINE PANKHURST

CAMPAIGNING FOR SUFFRAGE
Suffragettes went to great lengths
to advertise their cause, while also
shunning the constrictions of the
hated corset.

Flapper girls

1923

The all-black stage show *Runnin' Wild* introduces the charleston. Its flamboyant moves means girls need underwear that allows them to kick, gyrate and wriggle with ease.

After the trauma of the World War I, young women wanted to be as childish, outrageous and irresponsible as possible. Fashion echoed this mood. For women, a curvy shape was no longer de rigueur; breasts, hips, bottoms, thighs and bellies were all seriously unfashionable – the gawky adolescent look was the chic look. Curves were out; angles were in – and a new type of underwear was required.

Bright young things

They were the 'It' girls of their day; defined by their bobbed hair, plucked eyebrows and heavy, deliberate make-up. Their behaviour was considered shocking

TRENDSETTER
Silent movie star Louise Brooks became famous for her classic sleek bob and boyish figure.

and their fashion sense derided as ludicrous. They smoked, drank, spoke when they wanted to, and about whatever they wanted to, used slang and went out unchaperoned. But they looked amazing, they knew it and they had fun!

New freedom for women

Flapper girls were a product of the war. Women were allowed to work and have their own disposable income. They realized they no longer needed to stay at home and look

SHOWGIRLS

REVUE GIRLS
The dance style of the day meant that costumes had to be radically different from previous styles. Daring outfits displaying bare midriffs meant that the corset was no longer practical.

ANYTIME, ANYWHERE!
A dance first fashionable among the black population of South Carolina, the charleston was soon being danced at every opportunity all over the world.

Josephine Baker

Born Freda Josephine Carson in 1906 (she later took the name Baker from her second of four husbands), Josephine left a life of drudgery in 1919 to tour the United States in dance troupes. She later joined Sissle and Blake's production of *Shuffle Along*, and became an instant hit with audiences and the controversial heroine of the flapper generation. Josephine travelled to Paris and appeared in *Le Revue Negre*, where her uninhibited dancing and exotic costumes soon earned her the nickname 'Black Venus'. She continued the flamboyant act in her next show, *La Folie de Jour*, where she wowed audiences by wearing 16 bananas strung into a skirt, and was soon as famous for her daring attire as she was for her skin colour. Far more extravagant than any dancer seen before, Josephine brought the Jazz Age to Europe with a bang.

After appearing in the popular films *Zou Zou* (1934) and *Princess Tam Tam* (1935) and recording numerous songs, Josephine became a member of the French Resistance during World War II, smuggling secret messages on her song sheets, and was later an active member of the Civil Rights Movement. She died in 1974.

> " *Lovely,*
> *expensive*
> *and about*
> *nineteen.* "
>
> *F. SCOTT FITZGERALD*
> *(describing the flapper girl)*

FLAPPERS' UNDERWEAR
With the charleston craze sweeping the world, the embroidered knee-length flapper dress became essential wear. Attractive undergarments were created to be worn underneath, in pretty, feminine colours.

pretty. Refusing to retreat back into their kitchens when the men returned from the battlefields, the 1920s new women drove cars, rode bicycles and beat their menfolk at tennis and golf. Corsets wouldn't do. Their bras had to allow them to work and play with panache.

Bras to fit the fashion

Flapper girls also needed underwear to complement their distinct style of dressing. Corsets were *so* last decade! Bras needed to stop at the waist – or preferably above it – to allow a girl to don her scandalous new trousers. Under dance dresses, flappers wore a cylindrical one-piece, with suspenders attached; these flattened the breasts and hips and smoothed out the waist. The thin shoulder straps of many of the dance dresses led to a need for strapless bras, which began to be sold widely in 1926 and were given the catchy title of 'the no-shoulder-strap brassiere.' Many flappers hoped to create the illusion that underneath their dresses they were naked (shock, horror!).

Throughout the 1920s a variety of bras emerged, from those that covered the entire torso to much more skimpy strapless bras. The new found love of dancing and sport meant special sports underwear needed to be developed – in a traditional corset it had been almost impossible to bend at the waist. At the start of the decade, the 'corselette' was introduced, somewhere between a corset and bra. It wasn't perfect, but it was a start, giving women much greater ease of movement than before. By the end of the 1920s bust apparel was even neater, allowing the body more freedom than ever before.

No more cleavage

For the first time in living memory, Western women were freely displaying large areas of flesh – not the heaving cleavages of earlier centuries, but exposed

CURVES ARE OUT
The fashion of the day was to flatten the breasts, hips and waists as much as possible in order to achieve an androgynous figure. Special garments were available, claiming to make the flesh 'positively disappear'!

arms and legs. Women who would have been sex symbols in earlier times were now dismissed as fat. Bras were used to minimize and flatten the breasts but sometimes thick tape was used to bind them as close to the body as possible.

Popular bras

Because most flappers were young, most had smallish, firm breasts, untested by maturity, pregnancy, breast-feeding, or gravity. Bandeau-style bras – bought at department stores or made at home with a Butterick pattern – were popular. For those more generously endowed, a reducing bra, such as the popular Symington Side Lacer, was in order. The Symington was more substantial than most 'flapper bras,' but it needed its reinforcing to flatten bosoms. It featured lacing at both sides, which meant it could be pulled as tight as necessary to smooth away any bulging breasts.

NEW-FOUND FREEDOM
The arrival of bras enables young flappers to wear the new style of baggy trousers.

"*Nature made woman with a bosom, so why fight nature?*"

IDA ROSENTHAL

I dreamed I raced with the winds in my

maidenform bra

IT'S HERE!
CHANSONETTE
A fabulous American beauty of a bra!

MAIDENFORM
CHANSONETTE
WILL DO FOR
YOU WHAT
NO OTHER BRA
EVER COULD!

Lucky you! You may now experience the thrill of wearing a Chansonette bra for the very first time in your life! The women who already wear Chansonette wouldn't give it up for the world . . . in fact, they've made it the best selling, best loved bra in the world! What makes it so special? Spoke-stitched to round as it accentuates . . . it will do something for your contours you never dreamed possible! It's so delightfully comfortable too . . . you hardly know you're wearing it. And so easy to care for . . . washes in a wink with no pampering, wears for ages. Chansonette comes in your size and it's everything you've ever wanted in a bra. Don't put off the pleasure of trying Chansonette . . . you'll love it the minute you do!

Write for name of your nearest stockist

MAIDENFORM (LONDON) LIMITED Dept. N. 68 OXFORD STREET, LONDON,

✳ *It's quick . . . it's easy to buy your Chansonette in this ready-to-go package. It's in all better shops! Price 17/6*

Remember also to buy Maidenform's famous Pre-Lude, a dream of a bra with the amazing contour band that gives you that completely new kind of "under and up" lift . . . again only 17/6

MAIDENFORM AD, 1957
Maidenform went on to create one of the most successful advertising campaigns in advertising history: the famous 'I Dreamed' campaign.

A revolution in bra design

1927

A Maidenform brassiere advertisement appears in *Corset and Underwear Review*. The ad claims a 'double support pocket', better known as cups! The bra, as we now know it, had arrived.

In the 1920s, fashion had promoted the flat-chested look with the breasts bound against the chest wall. In contrast, Maidenform were now offering a brassiere designed to support the bust in a natural, uplifting position.

Quiet achiever

If ever a person was under-appreciated for her achievements, it is Ida Rosenthal. Any woman who has experienced the relief of finding a bra that truly fits, or of finding a shop that stocks bras in sizes larger than a C cup, should be thanking Ida – for it was she who invented the cup size, coming up with the sizes A, B, C and D. After this breakthrough, Ida and her husband, William, set up the Maiden Form Brassiere Company, which later became Maidenform – one of the world's most successful lingerie companies.

Genius at work

After spending long hours making an expensive dress, Ida was tired of seeing the carefully constructed line of her creations ruined by clients' clumsy underwear. Her solution was to begin custom-making bras, which she gave away free with each dress. The bras were a tribute to Ida's genius, each one tailored to fit each client with the minimum of obvious support, but actually providing great support from the strategic use of seams, darts, tucks and several well-placed snap fasteners.

The Biggest Selling Number In Brassieres Is
Now Fully Protected Against Imitators
U. S. PATENT HAS BEEN ISSUED FOR
The Maiden Form BRASSIERE
The Trade Is Warned To Sell Only The Genuine As Identified By The Above Label
And Here's Another That Is Selling Big
The **Maiden Form Decolleté**
ENID MFG. CO.
36 West 57th St., N. Y.
The **Maiden Form BRASSIERE**
The Original Uplift Brassiere

Big business

Soon, customers started sending in orders for the bras alone. The fame of Ida's wonderful creations had spread and new customers began arriving, wanting to be fitted for a bra that was comfortable and looked good. Ida realized she was onto a winner. Bras were such big business that she ended up selling Maidenform products in over 100 countries.

MAIDENFORM AD, 1927
This early Maidenform ad from *Corset and Underwear Review* celebrates the issue of a US patent for their famous backless bra.

A less scientific approach

Perhaps you've heard an old-time dressmaker refer to the 'fruit method' of bra measurements? This commonly labels A cups as 'half lemons,' B cups as 'half oranges,' C cups as 'half grapefruits' and D-cups as 'half melons'. What kind of melon has never been specified…

"Come up and see me sometime"

1932

Mae West becomes an instant celebrity after appearing in her first film *Night After Night*. Within two years of her Hollywood debut, she is earning the second-highest salary in America.

Although already an accomplished performer on Broadway, Mae West gained fame in Tinseltown almost entirely on the strength of her curvaceous figure. Hollywood didn't care that Mae had been selling out to fringe audiences in her outrageous one-woman shows. No, as far as the big producers were concerned, Mae had two overwhelming assets – and neither one of them was her sense of humour or prodigious talent for performing!

A girls' curves

By the time Mae West was stealing the show, short flapper dresses were old hat, as dress designers brought elegant hemlines down to the floor. But despite legs being covered, dresses now revealed arms, shoulders and vast expanses of the back, so bras were needed to accommodate every new fashion foible. Several new styles of bras were created – and these were more like bras that we'd recognize today. At last bras were being made to support,

No ANGEL
Voluptuous stars like Mae West took advantage of improving bras that both supported and separated large breasts.

separate and accentuate the breasts – in addition to bras worn with spaghetti-strapped and swooping backless dresses. With the arrival of stars like Mae West, bras were also being made to cater for large-breasted women.

Back to basics

Backless bras had straps that crossed over low in the back and tied round the waist, being fixed at the front with buttons. Okay, so they weren't exactly sexy when worn on their own, but the expensive dresses they were made to go beneath were breathtakingly seductive.

Betty Boo

Remember the precocious, curvaceous cartoon character Betty Boo? Her body was styled on Mae West's curves, and her outrageous antics – overtly sexual for that era – emulated West's own sexually liberated outlook. In one cartoon, Boo was seen to go topless. Not something cartoon characters were expected to do in puritanical, prohibition-era America!

ADOLPH ZUKOR
presents

MÆ WEST

in

"GOIN' TO TOWN"

"*You ought to get out of those wet clothes and into a dry martini.*"

MAE WEST

The Sweater Girls

1937

A pretty teenage blonde in a close-fitting cashmere sweater appears in a new film *They Won't Forget*. She becomes a major sensation and sets off another revolution in bra design.

LANA TURNER
An early publicity shot of the buxom Lana in her trademark cashmere sweater.

Mae West wasn't the only film star to win fame and fortune through her breasts. Teenage bombshell Lana Turner was the original Sweater Girl, although she hated the accolade. According to movie legend, she was 'discovered' in a café and was just fifteen when she began working on the film that was to make her name. In it, she played the small role of a murdered schoolgirl. Although Lana's face was undeniably pretty, it wasn't her sweet smile that caught the attention of the critics... it was her close-fitting sweater! Turner may have disliked her nickname, but it led to a glowing career in which she made over 50 films. She soon became one of the US forces' favourite pin ups – pictured, of course, in her trademark baby blue cashmere sweater – breasts ahoy!

" I made my first movie without ever considering that my walk-on role would be anything more than a one-time job. "

LANA TURNER

New bras for a new fashion

So, it was not only 1930s eveningwear fashions that were having an effect on the bra! Daytime fashions had also undergone a radical change, with women wearing close-fitting tops in cashmere (à la Lana Turner), crepe de Chine and jersey silks to complement their tweed suits and hip-hugging skirts. These tops required yet another revamp of bra design, one that showed off a woman's assets to their best advantage. The Sweater Girls were to influence fashion for another 20 years.

Bigger is better

The arrival of the Sweater Girl led to a new dilemma for women. In the late 1930s, women had the opposite problem from their counterparts in the 1920s who had agonized over their breasts being too large. Sweater Girl fashion meant that small-breasted women were now made to feel bad about their bodies and to seek for ways to make their assets more noticeable. Shortly after Lana Turner's debut, the first 'falsies' went on sale; these were pads made of moulded rubber that women wore inside their bras to give them the required Sweater Girl silhouette. They were developed by Warner's and nicknamed 'the gay deceivers'. These didn't become a huge commercial success until after the war, when falsies became BIG business.

STITCHED BRA
Bra manufacturers used circular stitching to give breasts the required shape.

Who wears the pants?

1939

After scandalizing Hollywood by refusing to pose for paparazzi and wearing slacks, Katharine Hepburn makes a sensational comeback and liberates women's fashion.

With the corset well and truly usurped by the bra, it was now possible for women to wear the pants – 'possible' but definitely not acceptable!

Leading ladies

The notorious flappers of the 1920s had donned their 'scandalous' trousers, but they were classed as 'rebellious young things' and the trend never went mainstream. It was not until the likes of Katharine Hepburn and Marlene Dietrich appeared in public in men's trousers that women began to consider wearing slacks in public. The 'Queen of Hollywood' has had a lasting impact on our ideas about 20th century womanhood.

Controversial Kate

Born in Connecticut, US, in 1907, Katharine Hepburn was one of Hollywood's most unique and enduring personalities. Her career as a Hollywood leading lady spanned seven decades; she starred in more than 50 quality films and won a record four Oscars for Best Actress. She always spoke her mind and had her own ideas about 'ladylike' behaviour. As a consequence, Hepburn's career suffered its share of ups and downs.

After a sensational debut in Hollywood, stories began to leak out of her unconventional behaviour

off-screen and her refusal to play the Hollywood game, always wearing slacks and refusing to wear make-up; never posing for pictures for the ubiquitous paparazzi and always refusing to give interviews or even sign autographs. Instead of applauding her independence, audiences were shocked and soon deserted her. From the period 1935 to 1938, she had just two hits and was labelled 'box-office poison'.

The Philadelphia Story

Hepburn responded with characteristic verve. She returned to New York to resume her acting career on Broadway, starring in the smash hit *The Philadelphia Story*. She bought the film rights and returned to Hollywood in 1939 determined to continue filmmaking on her own terms (including the right to choose her own co-stars and directors and wear whatever she darned well pleased).

Victory for women

As we shall see, the clothes worn by Hollywood stars had a huge impact on fashion. Hepburn was an unwitting ambassador for ready-to-wear clothing, which was practical, comfortable and cheap.

OUTSPOKEN STAR
Hepburn was the daughter of a doctor and suffragette. Her parents encouraged her to speak her mind, and she did just that.

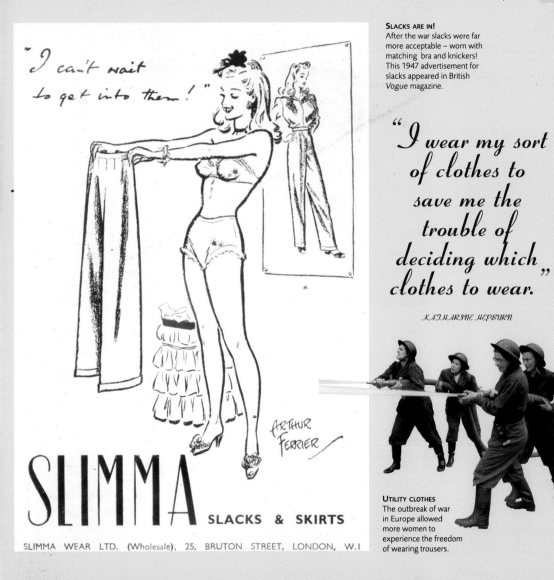

SLACKS ARE IN!
After the war slacks were far more acceptable – worn with matching bra and knickers! This 1947 advertisement for slacks appeared in British *Vogue* magazine.

"*I wear my sort of clothes to save me the trouble of deciding which clothes to wear.*"

KATHARINE HEPBURN

UTILITY CLOTHES
The outbreak of war in Europe allowed more women to experience the freedom of wearing trousers.

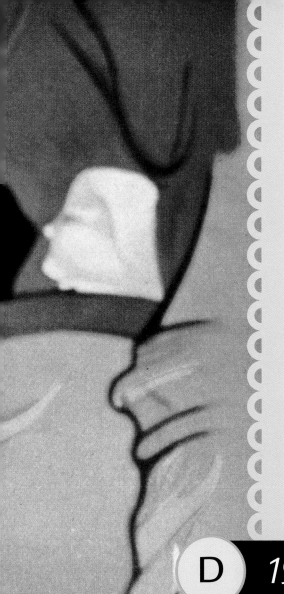

The Hollywood Years

The development of the bra continued unabated. This era saw the first proper padded bra; the return of corsets to go with Dior's 'New Look'; the first bikini; major developments in the design of strapless bras; cone-shaped cups to give the perfect Sweater Girl look; the first 'falsies'; the appearance of underwired bras and the introduction of new synthetic fabrics. Meanwhile, the 1950s underwear boutiques cashed in on the female desire to emulate the glamorous world of Hollywood stars.

D *1940–1959*

Making do

1941

In June, clothing rationing is introduced in Britain. Natural fibres such as cotton and silk are in seriously short supply, and British women are encouraged to 'make-do and mend'.

Under the new clothes rationing system, if you wanted to buy an item of clothing, you not only needed the money to do so, you also needed a certain amount of coupons.

Purchasing unmentionables

Every British citizen was issued with 66 coupons, which should have been enough to buy one complete outfit in a year (imagine – only buying one outfit in 12 months!). Although bras were not mentioned specifically in the government guidelines, three coupons were needed to buy 'other underclothing, including corsets' (presumably worded by an easily embarrassed male civil servant!).

In short supply

Ironically, on the same day that food rationing was introduced – 1 January 1940 – nylon first appeared in the UK but, unfortunately for women, all supplies were commandeered for war use, and it was not until the early 1950s that it was incorporated into bras.

In the US, the use of nylon was similarly restricted during the war but at least a certain amount was available to bra manufacturers. The synthetic material was popular because of its translucency in the form of the open-weave nylon marquisette. Rayon, another material popular with bra manufacturers, was also in short supply during and after the war and prices increased accordingly. The shortage of cotton continued after the war due to a poor crop yields in consecutive years 1946 and 1947.

WASTE NOT, WANT NOT
The 'Make-do and Mend' initiative encouraged British women to revamp old clothes and to use material from non-clothing items inventively, for example, making dresses out of old curtains.

Ve Can Do It!

ROSIE THE RIVETER
The US government encouraged women to take over jobs left vacant by the men. The inspirational Rosie was a fictional character, illustrated by Norman Rockwell, who rolled up her sleeves and got stuck in.

DESPERATE MEASURES
During the war, women painted their legs with dark paint to look like they were wearing stockings, which were in very short supply.

"Our women are serving actively in this war and they are doing a grand job."

ELEANOR ROOSEVELT

O FEB. 28

WAR PRODUCTION CO-ORDINATING COMMITTEE

Getting creative

Wartime governments introduced initiatives to encourage women to recycle old clothes and generally 'make do'. Bras were improvised – once again – from handkerchiefs and other scraps of material. Certain items useful for bra-making could be bought without coupons, these included elastic, tapes, braids, lace, net, ribbons and fabrics that were less than three inches wide.

Parachute silk was in high demand for making underwear, although it was difficult to come by. An airman falling out of the sky in your area would have meant free undies all round!

Pin-up girls

Meanwhile, servicemen stationed overseas and separated from their womenfolk were 'making do' with the 'pin-up girls'. The term pin-up girls was coined on 7 July 1941, by *Life* magazine, referring to the lingerie-clad, big-busted beauties whose endowments adorned barrack walls across the world. However, the term referred not only to the favourite Hollywood stars, such as Rita Hayworth, Ava Gardner and Betty Grable, but also to any attractive woman wearing little more than a sultry smile.

As vital as their role was during the war, the pin-up

girls who paraded around in their underwear were not the only women contributing to the war effort. Ordinary women were, once again, knuckling down to jobs left vacant by the men serving overseas. Many women enlisted in the armed forces. And, whereas in World War I women in the military were largely confined to cooking and cleaning, during World War II women handled anti-aircraft guns, ran the communications network, mended vehicles, and flew aeroplanes from one base to another.

Hollywood glamour

There was a revolutionary change in women's fashion after World War II. The returning troops wanted a pin-up girl to come home to. Women were tired of utility clothes and they too craved a touch of glamour. An exaggerated image of femininity was born that sexualized the hourglass figure but at the same time, paradoxically perhaps, promoted female 'innocence'. Dior's 1947 New Look spawned a need for underwear that was actually more confining than those worn during the war to help accomplish this new body shape. Women's relationship with their breasts was being re-invented in Hollywood's image. Think of the Monroe wiggle, encased in the curve-enhancing fashion that screamed a particular brand of blatant but 'encased' sexuality.

DOING THEIR BIT

RIVETING RITA

Rita Hayworth was as famous for her tempestuous love life as she was for her movie career. In 1941, Rita posed for a photograph wearing a low-cut, satin and lace nightdress. By the end of the war, the image had sold over five million copies!

DESIRABLE DOROTHY

Dorothy Lamour became famous after starring alongside Bing Crosby and Bob Hope in the 'road movies'. She was the first Hollywood starlet to volunteer to help sell war bonds, leading to her nickname 'the bond bombshell'.

> "There are two
> reasons why I'm in
> show business, and
> I'm standing on
> both of them."
>
> BETTY GRABLE

OUTRAGEOUS AVA
Although she kept the troops happy,
Ava Gardner caused scandal by
marrying Mickey Rooney with
a platinum wedding ring despite
the metal being in short supply.

BUBBLY BETTY
After a string of successful musicals Betty Grable became
a Hollywood hit. Her legs were insured for a million dollars.
Her popularity peaked during World War II, when she
was voted Number-One Pin-up Girl by US soldiers.

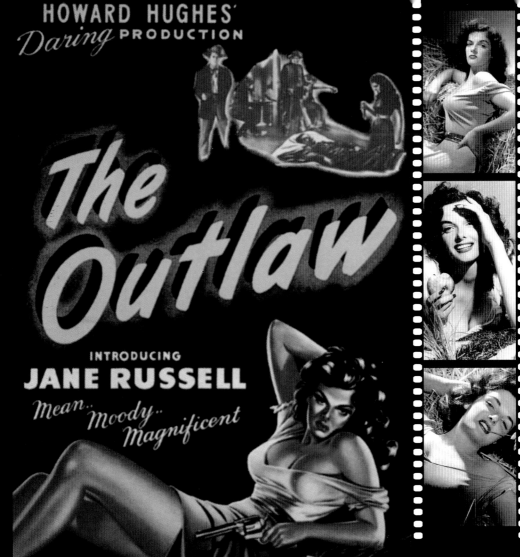

HOWARD HUGHES'
Daring PRODUCTION

The Outlaw

INTRODUCING
JANE RUSSELL

Mean.. Moody.. Magnificent

JACK BUETEL
THOMAS MITCHELL
WALTER HUSTON

RELEASED THROUGH UNITED ARTISTS

A STAR IS BORN
Jane Russell was promoted as a sultry new sex siren in her first film, *The Outlaw*, with cleavage revealed like never before!

The bra that saved Hollywood

1943

Howard Hughes 'engineers' the cantilever bra for the unknown actress Jane Russell. It ensures the success of his new movie and draws crowds back into the cinema after a wartime slump.

While other men were being conscripted into the military, the eccentric American billionaire Howard Hughes was scouring the length and breadth of the United States for a large-breasted actress. His quest ended when he found an unknown named Jane Russell, who was a US 38DD.

A feat of engineering

Hughes wanted Russell to star in his risqué 1940s western, *The Outlaw*. The role involved a lot of Russell pouting and spilling out of the top of her peasant blouse. The only problem was, her bra was too all-encompassing and didn't show enough cleavage. So Hughes, an experienced aviator and engineer, asked his personal staff of aeronautical engineers to put their skills towards developing the perfect half-cup bra with no noticeable seams – to make it look as though Russell wasn't wearing one. (Didn't these men know the world was at war?) Of course, being a DD cup, Russell couldn't actually go bra-less and still fall out of the top of her blouse – without any support her breasts would have been more likely to dangle down and appear beneath the bottom of it!

I dreamed I was

WANTED

in my Maidenform bra

A RUNAWAY SUCCESS
The Outlaw had a huge influence on bra fashion, with designs based on Jane Russell's bra in the film becoming hot sellers.

"The two and only Jane Russell."

BOB HOPE

Bad publicity works a treat

The resulting design became known as the 'cantilever bra', and gained a reputation as 'the bra that saved Hollywood'. Not surprisingly, given the current state of the world, Tinseltown had been suffering the effects of massive cutbacks. The publicity about the newly designed bra, and the lengths Hughes had gone to show off his new starlet's assets, brought the ailing movie town back into the headlines and the public returned to the cinema. Even better, in terms of publicity, was the outrage caused by the rumours of Russell's over-exposed breasts. And guess who started the furore? Howard Hughes. He told his employees to start phoning Christian ministers, housewives' groups and government departments concerned with 'family values', to complain about Hughes's 'lewd' and 'disgusting' film. The man was a genius.

Made in 1943, *The Outlaw* was banned by the censors but finally released in 1947, and ticket sales soared on account of its notoriety. The actress's breasts became the most famous in Hollywood.

BOND GIRL
Ursula Andress's
famous bikini from
the 1962 movie *Dr No*.

"This bikini made me a success."

URSULA ANDRESS

EXPLOSIVE REACTION
The bikini had a similar effect on the
fashion world to that of the bomb on
its namesake, Bikini Atoll.

INDECENT EXPOSURE
The always-daring Jayne Mansfield models a
seductive bikini in the 1950s. The bikini continued
to be considered daring for another 20 years.

Bikini bombshell

1946

Paris sees a milestone in bra history – the bikini makes its first appearance! The two-piece bathing suit is considered so shocking that only a nude cabaret dancer will model it.

Designed by a Frenchman, Louis Reard, the bikini derived its name from tiny Bikini Atoll, once a peaceful little island, but now the site of US bomb testing. In July 1946, two atomic bombs were exploded by the American military at Bikini Atoll. Reard commented that he had chosen the name because his invention would be as explosive to men as the bombs were to the Atoll.

Explosive entrance

Reard created his bikini from printed cotton. The two pieces used a total of 129 square inches of material. It was debuted on 5 July, just four days after the first atom bomb was detonated. The design on the bikini was of newsprint, a comment on the fact that its appearance was expected to explode into the media – and it certainly did that. After photographs of Micheline Bernardi, the cabaret dancer who first modelled the bikini, appeared in the papers, she received around 50,000 fan letters!

THE FIRST BIKINI
Micheline Bernardi makes a splash with the first bikini, which uses a newspaper print fabric designed to hit the headlines.

Too much for some

In 1947, a woman wearing a bikini on Venice Beach was arrested for indecent exposure – the following day most papers carried a photograph of her being led away by the police in handcuffs! Throughout the 1950s and 1960s, the bikini was still considered outrageous in most quarters and relatively few women bought them, although some experimented with making bikinis at home. In 1950, a London housewife was brave enough to sunbathe on Hampstead Heath in a homemade bikini. Upon being spotted by the police, she was ordered to cover up instantly!

Bikinis and Bond girls

In the end, it was Hollywood, once again, that changed fashion history. Once the big-name movie stars started wearing bikinis, vast throngs of women in the Western world started to follow their example. Perhaps the biggest impact on the history of the bikini was made in 1962 by Swiss actress Ursula Andress. The white, belted, hipster bikini that Andress wore in the first James Bond film, *Dr No* (see opposite page), not only sent sales of two-piece swimwear skyrocketing, it also made Andress an international celebrity. The scene has been emulated in a myriad of movies ever since, but never bettered.

Dior's 'New Look'

1947

With much fabric still in short supply, Christian Dior unveils a daring new collection. His outfits require yards of exquisite cloth. Governments are furious at the extravagance, but women adore it.

With the war over, clothing rationing was starting to come to an end. Women in the forces were longing to hang up their uniforms and, after years of making do, mending and 'utility clothing', women were equally keen to dress up and be frivolous. Their prayers were answered by French fashion designer Christian Dior.

The hourglass figure

The 'New Look' was a celebration of the hourglass figure. There were no shoulder pads or suppressed hip lines here; instead the collection employed smooth curves, nipped-in waists, skirts that flowed out over the hips (under which billowed voluminous petticoats) and bodices that required naturally rounded and perky breasts – preferably large ones.

Corsets make a return

Feminists were angered because Dior's fashion meant a reversion to the corset. By now, however, corsets were no longer the health-endangering items of Victorian times, thanks to huge advances in synthetic materials, more innovative styles of dress-making and improved medical understanding

of the body. A woman who felt cheated by nature could achieve a divine New Look silhouette with the aid of a new-look corset and many women perceived the underwear as sexy and empowering – albeit still restrictive of movement.

Tricks of the trade

Not all women became newly enamoured of the corset, however, and some chose to wear just a new uplifting bra, knickers and suspenders. Others, who felt they needed extra help, chose a complicated collection of underwear, all of which targeted different body areas. To achieve the desired 'nipped-in' waist, a type of corselette was made, nicknamed a 'waspie'. Above this was worn a special bra, invented to lift the breasts higher than nature had intended. These bras helped women in their forties look as though they had retained the perky breasts of adolescence. Women whose hips were naturally slim attached stomach and hip pads to their petticoats, and women whose breasts were small used cotton wool or other wadding to pad out their bodices.

DIOR UNDERWEAR
To complement his 'New Look', Dior created new lingerie that flattered the figure.

LADIES OF LUXURY
For this outfit, Dior emphasized post-war decadence by using satin and embroidering with gold and diamonds.

"There is nothing I would like better than to make every woman look and feel like a Duchess."

CHRISTIAN DIOR

Setting the trend

The 'New Look', and the resulting impact on 1950s designers such as Norman Hartnell, led to the reintroduction and reinvention of the strapless bra. These allowed women to show off their shoulders to their best advantage in Dior's elegant new gowns.

Bras of the big screen

1955

The cone-shaped bra achieves fame after being championed by the film stars Marilyn Monroe and Brigitte Bardot. Every aspiring sweater girl has to have one.

By the early 1950s, bras were not just uplifting and separating, they were also unnaturally shaped. For some reason, fashion had decreed that the sexiest shape for a woman's breasts was to be pointy!

A new breed of bras

The new breed of sweater girls, notably Brigitte Bardot, Diana Dors, Jayne Mansfield and Marilyn Monroe, wore bras and dresses that forced the breasts into a cone shape. The cup shape was achieved by circular stitching that went all around the cups, from top to bottom (an idea Madonna was to revive in later years). This new breed of bra had actually been around since 1939, but its development was postponed by the outbreak of World War II. At the start of the 1950s, the shape of the bra had been only mildly conical, but soon the fashion world decided that the more pointy the better, and bras with specially stiffened points were invented. As the 1950s progressed, bra manufacturers began mass-producing bras, allowing women to purchase the same bust shapes seen on Hollywood celebrities and advertised in magazines. Increased use of nylon and elastics ensured unprecedented comfort. Indeed, advertisements from the time often mention comfort in connection with a particular bra, and the word became a popular part of bra names at the time.

Accentuate your assets

When Maidenform released its bestselling 'Chansonette' bra in the UK, they ran an advert in *Vogue*: 'What makes it so special? Spoke-stitched to round as it accentuates ... it

CO-STARRING...

DIANA DORS
A sexy British blonde, Diana Dors will forever be known for her billing as the 'English Marilyn Monroe'. However, Diana began her career long before Marilyn, and proved to be a fine actress, although often typecast as a 'gold-digging blonde'. Her film-acting career, which began in the 1940s, lasted well into the 1980s.

SOPHIA LOREN
For a woman whose early career was based mostly on her measurements (38C), Sophia Loren carved out an award-winning acting career, wrote books, launched a line of perfume and eyewear, and became an icon of the cinema who is adored by millions of fans the world over.

> "*A photographer once told me that my two best points are between my waist and my neck.*"
>
> *MARILYN MONROE*

Mass-produced bras

To acquire that 1950s hourglass look, women gave up making their own underwear and started buying the mass-produced 'bullet' bras. In order to reduce costs, manufacturers outsourced part of the production process to foreign facilities with cheaper labour. Bra makers in the US outsourced labour to countries such as Mexico and the Philippines.

MARILYN MONROE
Like Mae West before her, Marilyn Monroe famously wore specially created corsets that pushed her breasts up and out. It wasn't simply the fact that she deliberately wore one heel slightly shorter than the other that gave her that much-imitated bum-wiggle, it was also that her underwear was slightly restrictive in order to keep her shoulders well back and her breasts well forwards, and to make her work just that little bit harder when she walked.

will do something for your contours you never dreamed possible! It's so delightfully comfortable too ... you hardly know you're wearing it.'

The iconic corset

Meanwhile, the corset (which never claimed to be comfortable!) had made its comeback with Dior's New Look and was once again an established part of a woman's wardrobe. By the mid-1950s, it wasn't something she necessarily wore all day, but it was an essential under a sexy, curvaceous evening dress, with its nipped in waist and exaggeratedly pointed bodice. Corsets had also become an accepted male fantasy, regularly worn by titillating models in magazines such as *Playboy*. The corset was no longer a symbol of female oppression; it was now well on its way to iconic status and had already partially evolved into a symbol of feminine power and domination.

Hollywood legends

And the inspiration behind all this glamour and clamour? In the 1950s, the leading ladies of Hollywood enjoyed unprecedented fame and had a huge influence on fashion. After *The Outlaw*, in which Jane Russell famously launched her fabulous 38DD figure, she proved herself as an actress and appeared alongside Marilyn Monroe in the classic comedy *Gentlemen Prefer Blondes*

(1953). The two superstars were famously photographed making hand (and breast) impressions in concrete slabs for Hollywood's Walk of Fame. And Marilyn Monroe? – well, the name speaks for itself. She has still not been eclipsed – and she was only a C cup! (34C to be precise, according to her dressmaker.)

Teen idols

By the mid-1950s, however, Monroe and Russell had had their heyday and a host of new stars appeared in the Hollywood firmament. First among them was Natalie Wood. The slender star (a mere 32B!) was one of Hollywood's hottest properties, and she paved the way for less curvaceous teen idols.

A child star who had found fame in the 1940s at the age of nine, in the film *Miracle on 34th Street*, Natalie Wood went on to become one of America's best-loved stars (although, sadly, she was also one of the most troubled), and appeared with James Dean in the 1955 blockbuster *Rebel Without a Cause*. Her girl-next-door looks afforded her the kind of innocent star quality Doris Day enjoyed; a refreshing change for many American cinemagoers from the school of platinum-blonde, big-boobed starlets. Wood was a precursor to the super-elegant Audrey Hepburn, whose trim figure (a waif-like 34A) was a world away from the pumped-up Mansfield, Monroe, Dors and Russell wanabees.

CO-STARRING...

BRIGITTE BARDOT
French sex kitten Brigitte Bardot (35B) scandalized – and thrilled – American audiences in the mid-1950s after going several steps further than Jane Russell had done and appearing naked on screen. Her silhouette became as famous in America as in her native France and her name remains synonymous with the hourglass figure and the bikini.

GINA LOLLOBRIGIDA
Tagged 'The Most Beautiful Woman in the World' after her signature movie in 1955, 'La Lollo' was the archetypal Italian beauty. Her short 'tossed salad' hair was especially influential. (In fact, there's a type of curly lettuce named 'Lollo' in honour of her cute hairdo.)

I dreamed I was a social butterfly

in my maidenform bra

THE HOLLYWOOD DREAM
Bra manufacturers Maidenform enticed women to
buy into the Hollywood dream with this glamorous
1955 advertisement for a fashionable bullet bra.

Bust boosters

1958

The first push-up bikini arrives at Frederick's of Hollywood. With the iconic status now afforded to Sweater Girls, bust support and enhancement for women is big business.

While some women resorted to breast enlargement surgery, most were content to fake it. Of course, many women simply improvised with the timeless technique of stuffing handkerchiefs into an oversized bra. But bra manufacturers were quick to offer more hi-tech solutions with padded bras sporting names like Secret Charm and Curves 2-U.

Booster bras

Maidenform provided bras with removable pads that were inserted into specially designed pockets, but most booster bras had the foam-rubber padding stitched permanently into the cups. The Trés Secrète bra went a couple of steps further and included an inflatable insert that could be blown up with a 'discreet' plastic straw.

Eveningwear bras

However, if daytime fashion of the 1950s was dominated by snug-fitting sweater sets and increasingly pointy breasts accentuated by the bullet bras, eveningwear exposed more and more flesh. Demi-cup and strapless bras were a must for revealing eveningwear, both styles accommodating the bow-necked – often shoulderless or off-the-shoulder – fashions made increasingly popular by Hollywood.

Strapless-bra patents outnumbered all other styles during the 1950s, all designs including some form of wire framing. The wire was originally designed to increase support for large-breasted women, but customers and manufacturers

alike were quick to cotton on to the fact that the rigidity of the underwire enhanced the assets of small-breasted women by thrusting them up to new heights.

BLOW-UP BOOBS!
Lingerie companies came up with innovative ways of increasing women's bust sizes, such as this inflatable strapless bra, to be blown up with a plastic straw.

Jayne Mansfield

Despite making only one successful film, Mansfield remains one of the most instantly recognizable Sweater Girls – and it's all down to having huge breasts and a voracious appetite for publicity stunts. These stunts included 'stranding' herself on a desert island, 'accidentally' losing her bikini top in front of a wall of paparazzi and posing naked for *Playboy* in 1957. The hungry starlet knew she had achieved her desire to become the new Jane Russell after being photographed in a red bikini alongside the headline 'Jayne outpoints Jane'. Ouch! Catfight anyone? In short, Jayne Mansfield was famous for being famous and for having big boobs.

Frederick's of Hollywood

One of the most influential names in the creation of the 1950s silhouette was that of an ex-GI, Frederick Mellinger. During the war years, Mellinger and his buddies did a lot of wistful talking about their wives and girlfriends and what kind of lingerie turned them on (hey, it was wartime, they needed a diversion). So when he left the army, Mellinger moved west from Manhattan to set up a lingerie store in Hollywood, catering to Hollywood stars who relied on Frederick's for great quality, fantastic fit and a sexy look that embodied Hollywood glamour. By the end of the 1950s, women were going to Frederick's for a total makeover – from high heels to wigs, pads to minimizers.

> # "Dramatic art in her opinion is knowing how to fill a sweater."
>
> BETTE DAVIS, ON JAYNE MANSFIELD

JAYNE MANSFIELD
Apparently, when Mansfield met The Beatles, she asked John Lennon if his hair was real. Quick as a flash, Lennon replied, 'Are those for real?'

The 'real' deal

Thankfully, times have changed since the days of the inflatable bra and, although there may be a few women still using their husband's socks to create a cleavage, today's technology provides a more natural-looking solution. Frederick's of Hollywood created the first realistic silicone-filled breasts, which slot into a specially designed bra and look, feel and move just like the real things, even warming to body temperature. Obviously popular with less well-endowed women, Frederick's breasts are apparently also a hit with cross-dressing men.

The Pop Years

These were decades of flux, to be sure. From a fashion standpoint, the 1960s saw everything from beatniks to go-go dancers to hippies, new synthetics to day-glo colours, to an obsession with natural and ethnic fabrics. The 1970s was equally interesting, with its succession of browns and suede to its jewel-toned disco satin to the punk pvc, rips and safety pins. Just as you'd probably expect, bra fashions of this time were a reflection of these fashion trends, but comfort was largely the key.

DD *1960–1979*

"The bra has joined the lipstick and heels in becoming one of the beloved symbols of growing up."

MERCY DOBELL

SHOPPING SPREE
Knowing the Baby Boomers had more money to spend than their wartime predecessors, bra manufacturers began to target the teen market with adverts they could relate to.

For the smoothest shape this side of a sweater

Lovable *Seam-Free** sweater bra

Yes, Lovable does away with seams to give your figure the smoothest, roundest, youngest shaping *under all!* The secret? The cups, pre-shaped with foam, are covered with the softest all-nylon stretch Helanca. Sides and bands are cotton. In a rainbow of colors: red, pink, blue, black or white. Only $1.50 • Also in luxurious nylon lace Helanca. $2.50

Insert: Smooth combination, color-matched to your SEAM-FREE Sweater Bra. "Sweetheart" panty girdle slims you lightly, firmly, smoothly. Nylon stretch Helanca and rubber. One size fits all. Red, pink, blue, black or white. Only $2 • In long leg panty girdle. $3

only $1⁵⁰

IT COSTS SO LITTLE TO LOOK LOVABLE
The Lovable Brassiere Co., New York 16 • Los Angeles 16 • Sold everywhere in the United States, Canada and throughout the world. Ask for Lovable girdles, too.

*U.S. PATENT #2857916

Targeting teens

1964

There are almost 12 million teenage Baby Boomers in the US alone. Bra manufacturers target this lucrative new market, with an offering of specially designed teen bras.

As a product of the post-war 'Baby Boom', there was an unprecedented number of teenagers at the start of the 1960s. There was no famine, war, pestilence, disease, or even high unemployment rates for families to worry about. Plus, teens were better off financially than ever before. All this meant more leisure time to spend that extra money – mostly on clothes. Teenagers became an important market – in the US alone, they spent $85 million dollars on bras. Bra advertisements of the 1960s specifically targeted teens in a variety of ways.

SWEET 16
With more freedom than ever before, the 1960s teenager wanted to be seen as more grown up. Maidenform tapped into this desire with the Undertone bra, promising to shape and define the youthful figure.

Daisy

Daisy by Permalift took the instructional approach, asking magazine readers 'When Should You Start Wearing a Bra?' The advertisement goes on to answer just that, reassuring teens that '...maybe now is not too soon' for a Daisy bra, while coaxing young women to 'tell your mother about them and ask her to go in with you to a fitting. It'll be fun.'

Undertone

Remember those ubiquitous Maidenform adverts, where ladies dreamed they were doing whatever while wearing their skivvies? Wanting to include the teen market, Maidenform created the Undertone bra, and created ads exactly like their adult ones, with bra-clad high school students dreaming about being 'wild in the west' or some such thing. The best line in the magazine ad? 'Undertone makes the most of the young figure. Each cup is edged with firm embroidery that holds the bra snug as it shapes and defines your curves. (The best definition of curves since algebra was invented.)'

Qform

Mary Quant was the UK's fashion darling, associated with the minidress, make-up and even undies. Quant recognized that teenagers wanted a look radically different from their parents and designed the Qform bra for the 1960s youth, a demi-cup, push-up in a range of shades, decorated with the Mary Quant posy and typifing her simplistic, athletic style.

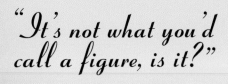

A NEW YOUTHFULNESS
Twiggy was a natural model and
the perfect 1960s shape: narrow
body, perfect square shoulders,
long legs and small bust.

Twiggy: the original waif

1966

A waif-thin teenager, Leslie Hornby, is named the 'Face of 1966' by Britain's *Daily Express*. She develops into a fashion catalyst and the first supermodel is born.

In March 1965 Leslie met Nigel Davies, a popular mod working in a hair salon. Nigel, realizing Leslie's potential, became her boyfriend, manager and agent, changing his name to Justin de Villeneuve. He renamed Leslie 'Twiggy', referring to her waif-like figure (her measurements were 5ft 4in, 90lbs and 32-22-32 when she began modelling). The plan certainly worked because two weeks into her career, Twiggy was booked solid and she went on to become the world's highest-paid model of the 1960s.

Conical bras hit the dust

Twiggy, the childlike Brit with the doe eyes and the gamine-crop hairdo has been called the original waif. Somehow, the exaggerated, clown-like make-up and quasi-skeletal figure spoke of a ground-breaking aesthetic that captured the times perfectly. She was the first model to become a celebrity virtually overnight with her boyish looks and figure. This look was a bold departure from the curvy female forms of the previous decades – 1950s, 1940s and 1930s – with their obvious, highly separated, often conical bosoms. Instead, Twiggy's flat-chested figure was the ideal role model for women about to go braless in the late 1960s; her 32-inch breasts needed no support under her trademark shift dresses and she became an icon of the 1960s cultural revolution.

Twiggy branches out

Twiggy was just 15 when she first started modelling, but retired only four years later (it was said she was suffering from burnout). Shortly following her retirement from modelling, she launched a career in acting and singing and played alongside Ken Russell in the hit movie *The Boyfriend*. She won two Golden Globes in 1971 for Best Actress and Most Promising Newcomer.

Barbie

In 1967, Mattel released a Twiggy Barbie doll in response to the huge popularity of the diminutive icon who was elemental in creating the lanky, flat silhouette that was so popular in the mid to late 1960s.

Originating from a racy German 1950s comic strip, Barbie is the best-selling doll in the world today, sold in 140 countries at a rate of two dolls every second.

Some say Barbie made girls comfortable with the idea of puberty, growing into a woman, getting breasts and so forth. Others argue that the doll was a powerful catalyst for eating disorders and poor body image among teenagers and young women. The same criticism has been levelled at Twiggy, Kate Moss and the waifs of the 1990s. In fact, the pressure to be thin is still very much present at the start of the 21st century.

Bra burners

1968

A group of protesting women gather in Atlantic City, New Jersey, right outside the venue in which a Miss America pageant is taking place.

Weary of being second-class American citizens (earning less than half of what men earned for comparable work, being discriminated against in education and careers, and more), a group of women in Atlantic City decided to make a statement. Something big. Knowing how much attention bras (and breasts) received in the US, they decided to make a bonfire of brassieres and a few other constricting feminine items, such as girdles, panty-hose, high-heeled shoes and the like.

ANTI-BRA PROTEST, 1969
Another demonstration takes place outside a department store in San Francisco, California.

The burning bra myth

While popular lore has the Atlantic City women removing their bras in public, tossing them into a trash can and igniting them, historians believe this never happened. Apparently, unable to get a fire permit, the women went ahead with their protest but could only make the gesture of throwing the bras into a trash can. Subsequently, there may have been bra bonfires in towns across the US. What *were* burned were draft cards and flags in protest of the Vietnam War. Some experts suggest that the bras in the trash can and the torched draft cards may have merged in popular memory to create the mind's eye image of a flaming brassiere.

For many women, bra burners had turned the bra into a visual symbol of gender oppression, while introducing the idea of going braless as a way to enjoy physical comfort above meeting social expectations.

Braless women

In the 1960s, going without a bra was as radical as wearing one just a few decades earlier. Still, discarding the bra was an important step, allowing women to put their own physical comfort over society's collective discomfort with loose breasts.

SUMMER LOVE
Hippies, here seen at Glastonbury music festival in the UK, were among the first to free themselves of the bra. The whole hippie movement gave many women freedom of choice – to wear a bra or not.

Barbarella

Jane Fonda played the sexy sci-fi character Barbarella in the 1968 classic film. It is the 41st century, and Barbarella receives a call from the President of Earth. It seems a diabolical scientist is threatening to end universe-wide peace. Naturally Barbarella restores order, losing at least one piece of her skimpy outfit per scene in the process. Fonda's character wears many intriguing bra-like garments, celebrating the female form – more specifically, the female breasts.

Bralessness was a gradual process, one that was furthered by a host of events, from the hippies to the 'bra burners' to the breast-feeding movement. Once Americans – or at least the younger ones – were used to seeing natural breasts for the soft, swaying appendages they really were, people became more accepting of seeing breasts unbound and moving freely under clothing.

In effect, braless women gave women a choice – to wear a bra or not. Moreover, the braless trend encouraged lingerie companies to lure braless females back into the underwear-wearing fold by creating more comfortable bras, with more natural silhouettes (see next page). Most women would agree that this isn't such a bad thing at all. And we still have that choice today.

Soft and natural

1970

In France, the innovative Huit Company introduces the first moulded bra. It gives women a more natural look but the trend only lasts a few years –

Taking advantage of the increasing demand for more natural, less supportive bras, the early 1970s saw a spate of seamless, see-through bras being produced.

Skintones are in!
Gone were the garish colours and prints of the 1960s, to be replaced by ecru, beige, peach, apricot, buff, tan, brown and other complexion-copying neutrals. And while white bras still existed, they were now competing with these flesh-toned shades.

A softer feel
Natural was the hold of choice for the moment, perfect for creating a 'better than braless' silhouette. Underwire, heavy stitching, stiff panels and other supportive devices fell out of favour, especially among younger and more fashion-conscious women. The styles of the day were softer and less structured than those seen in the 1950s and 1960s. Thanks to new lightweight spandex blends and new methods of creating seamless cups, women got the bras they wanted.

Although smaller, perkier breasts were the ideal for these type of bra, as the decade wore on it became apparent that women in the UK, Europe, North America and elsewhere

SMALL PACKAGES
Small, pert breasts were ideally suited to the sheer, simple bras of the 1970s, although the lack of support proved harder for those women blessed with a bigger cleavage.

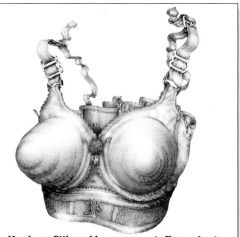

Here's one little problem we can get off your chest.

We know you and your bra have your little differences. When you're running around it's creeping about. And when you're dancing, it's twisting.

Consider, if you will, the advantages of a Pretty Polly Body Stocking.

You'll never fall out with it.

It doesn't push you around like a bra. Because it doesn't have straps or buckles or bones.

And it doesn't show up any lumps and bumps you don't already have.

In fact, a Pretty Polly Body Stocking can hardly be seen at all. (Our five muted tones include one called 'nude').

To think, it can relieve you of all these little hang ups for a tiny 9/-. *Recommended retail price*

PP PRETTY POLLY

A Pretty Polly Body Stocking is like no other underwear.

were getting bustier (due at least in part to the Pill). Companies responded by expanding their lines to a size DD or larger.

Cheap labour

Such was the fashion for going braless started by the hippy and feminist movement that many lingerie manufacturers went out of business or turned their attention to reducing production costs. Starting in the early 1970s, bras that used to be made and sold in the United States were sent overseas – to the Philippines, Hong Kong, Jamaica, Honduras, Mexico, Dominican Republic – to be sewn by cheap contract labour. Typically, a small component of the bra, maybe its clasp or a label, was sewn onto the finished garment by US workers, thus allowing the item to be marked as 'Made in the USA'.

Black models

In a reflection of improving racial equality in the US, Lovable, Exquisite Form, Bestform, Delightform, Glamorise, Lilyette, Formfit Rogers and Gossard began using dark-skinned models (though many of them were Caucasians with good tans) for bra advertisements placed in African-American interest magazines and newspapers; even in some mainstream publications.

> "*I burned my bra but it took the fire department four days to put it out.*"
>
> *DOLLY PARTON, ON HER UNFASHIONABLY LARGE BREASTS*

SEAMLESS SILHOUETTE
Soft, natural bras gave women the freedom to wear what they wanted without unsightly bulges or restrictive clasps and straps.

The Kicky-Dicky

When it came to 1970s underwear, less was definitely more. Women were demanding a bra that looked and felt natural, or which gave a feel of not having a bra on at all.

Gelmart came up with the ideal solution. The Kicky-Dicky was a cropped top made from nylon which needed no bra because the support was built in. For the young and daring, the top could be worn on its own, although it looked just as good under a sweater.

Otto Titzling!

1971

A book published this year provides a whole new version of the invention of the bra. Although the work is clearly farcical, it gains universal status as the truth.

There is a popular belief that it was not Mary Phelps Jacob who invented the bra, but a man named Otto Titzling, who beat Mary to it by just one year. This story, however, is apocryphal, based on the book published in 1971, featuring a cast of dubiously named characters. Incredibly, the story has become accepted.

A LIKELY STORY
According to Wallace Reyburn, Otto Titzling invented the bra in 1912 when he was sharing a boarding house with an Icelandic opera singer blessed with an uncommonly large bust.

A cunning work of fiction

The book, by antipodean author Wallace Reyburn, was entitled *Bust Up: The Uplifting Tale of Otto Titzling and the Development of the Bra*. It tells the story of a young German whose desire to invent the bra was inspired by his father's work as a bridge building engineer. His two brothers join their father in civil engineering, whereas Otto follows his uncle into the fashion trade, where he is determined to make his name in innovative corsetry. After an argument with his father about his eccentric choice of career, Otto moves to New York where he rooms in the same boarding house as a large-busted Icelandic opera singer, for whom he finally has the opportunity to invent his first bra, in 1912.

When Hans met Lois

The story continues with Otto meeting his business partner – the aptly named Hans Delving – after World War I. The pair then encounter a Swedish athlete, with the ironic name of Lois Lung, who needs Otto to invent her a pair of 'inflatable falsies' to protect her breasts when hurdling. This is how the first sports bra was created! (If none of these names seems odd to you, try saying them out loud!)

OOOH MATRON!
The British *Carry On* films, popular in the 1960s and 1970s, were famous for their endless innuendo, and the cheap gags were as farcical as those in Wallace Reyburn's book.

Wearing a 'titzling'!

In the late 1920s, the flamboyant Philippe de Brassiere arrives in New York. He is a dastardly dress designer from Paris who claims he invented the brassiere first – hence the name – and takes Otto to court. Because Otto has failed to patent his invention, de Brassiere wins the case and, as the author explains, that's why the garment became known as a 'brassiere' instead of a 'titzling'. Wallace Reyburn also wrote a book about the man who invented the flushing loo. It is called *Flushed with Pride: The Story of Thomas Crapper*.

Bee-stings or bazookas?

The list of euphemisms for breasts, large and small, is apparently endless. Here's just a small handful of them.

Slang for big boobs			Slang for small boobs	
Airbags	Feeding bottles	Knockers	Bee-stings	Fried eggs
Balloons	Funbags	Melons	Berries	Kittens' noses
Baps	Gazongas	Party tits	Chapel hat pegs	Mosquito bites
Bazookas	Hooters	Puppies	Cherries	Smiddys
Bongos	Honkers	Shock absorbers	Diddies	Two raisins on a
Coconuts	Jugs	Shoulder boulders	Eyes	breadboard

Agent Provocateur

Vivienne Westwood's son, Joseph Corré, and Serena Rees opened the first Agent Provocateur in London's Soho in 1994 amid a blaze of publicity. It was the first shop of its kind to provide glamorous and tantalizing lingerie for the female form without embarrassment or shame.

Agent Provocateur strongly believes in the absolute uniqueness of the feminine form. Their customers range from rock stars, supermodels and actresses to strippers, housewives and businessmen. Signature pieces of underwear have been displayed in numerous international exhibitions,and you also may have seen one of their controversial cinema commercials. They've certainly put the passion back into lingerie! Featured left is the saucy Diva Lace corset – hot or what?

Shock wave

1976

Malcolm McLaren dresses the British punk-rock band The Sex Pistols in clothes designed by Vivienne Westwood. The British public is scandalized by the shocking new look.

Rock purists will for ever be arguing about punk rock: Did it start in New York or London? 1975 saw the launch of the New York magazine *Punk* chronicle the new music – by Iggy Pop, The Ramones, Richard Hell, et al. – coming out of clubs such as CBGB and Max's Kansas City. But it is unarguably the Brits who were responsible for the clothing style that we now call punk. The purposely ripped clothing, provocative T-shirts, bondage trousers, Doc Marten boots, day glo-coloured hair, spiky coifs, theatrical make-up, body piercings and so on can be traced back to London, where Malcolm McLaren and Vivienne Westwood had a clothing shop called Sex.

Aggressive underwear

McClaren, who had been in New York managing the New York Dolls, returned to the UK to launch The Sex Pistols, the band most closely associated with the punk movement. Whereas hippies celebrated sex as free love, the UK punks used sex as an aggressive in-your-face kind of way to shock those around them. Thus T-shirts often had suggestive slogans or even pictures of naked breasts, cowboys, or whatever. It wasn't uncommon to see toplessness as part of a night-time costume and bondage-style bras, such as open-breasted styles, were often the sole piece of clothing a female punk would wear above the waist.

The future of fetish

The legacy of all this? After years spent draping the body in natural fabrics or shiny disco cloth, the world was forced to see fashion in a very different way. Furthermore, the general public was introduced to a considerable amount of fetishwear, much of which was absorbed by the culture at large and incorporated into everyday lingerie, street fashion and even eveningwear.

SEX, DRUGS AND PUNK
By 1976, Vivienne Westwood's daring fetish gear was an integral part of the punk scene. Contemporaries such as pop star Chrissie Hynde and writer Alan Jones hung out and even worked at her shop, Sex, helping to make her a true fashion icon.

THAT DRESS
Liz Hurley claims that she only wore her punk-inspired Versace dress to the 1994 *Four Weddings and a Funeral* premiere because there were no others left in their press office. Hmmm - a happy coincidence perhaps or an extremely clever piece of self-marketing?

The Wonder Years

These two decades were the most exciting bra time ever. The 1980s and 1990s were two very different decades: we saw bra fashion move from glamour and sport to heroin chic, then on to the glorious re-emergence of the cleavage. There were constant innovations. It seemed as if something new – from fabrics to fillers to bust silhouettes – came along every week. The over-the-top 1980s and anything-goes 1990s made for some interesting bustlines, each of which required its own type of support, as you will see!

E *1980–1999*

More, more, more

1981

The American glamour soap *Dynasty* is screened. Characters sport huge shoulder pads, ever-expanding hair and lavish underwear – diamante-encrusted teddies with opulent use of lace.

Dynasty set the style for the 1980s. It was a decade of MORE. Hair had more body – lots more in some cases – thanks to permanent waves and industrial-strength styling products. Clothes had more oomph, make-up was in brighter colours and applied more thickly, people wore more and bigger earrings, and bodies – bustlines included – were firmer than they'd ever been. The 1980s was the decade of luxury lingerie, to make you look and feel good. There was glamour, opulence and suddenly a lot more choice. Bras started to be manufactured using different materials: velvet, satin and silk imitations incorporating Lycra, polyesters and jersey materials in a huge range of styles and designs.

SHAMELESSLY SEXY
Suddenly women were 'it', holding the reins in the boardroom and the bedroom. Power dressing on the outside with confident, sexy lingerie underneath.

Our cups runneth over

The 1980s was the decade to think BIG: big hair, big shoulder pads, big make-up, big salaries, and best of all big boobs. And if God didn't bestow blinding knockers on you, don't worry, think big implants.

If you've ever stuffed a pair of socks into your bra, worn falsies or bought a bra so padded that it's bulletproof, then somewhere that desire to literally build up what you've got has taken hold. During the 1980s, a growing number of women were dispensing with these add-on methods and going for the daddy of all enhancements – implants. Yes, that's major surgery to get turbo-charged superhooters.

Boob jobs

Silicone gel implants have been around since the early 1960s, but the fashion for having 'boob jobs' only gained serious popularity in the 1980s. However, problems with implants kept grabbing the headlines and, in 1992, silicone gel implants were banned in the US. Since then, saline implants have been the method of choice. Despite continuing bad press, breast enlargement is still the most common cosmetic procedure performed on women in the UK, and the second most popular cosmetic procedure (after liposuction) for women in the US.

What did the boob job do for the bra? Well, it boosted bra sales as millions of women donated their old B cup bras to charity shops and splashed out on luxury DD bras to further enhance their enhancements.

GLAMOUR SOAPS
The glam years of
the 1980s were
perfectly symbolized
by the extravagances
of *Dynasty* (left)
and *Dallas*.

Let's get physical

1982

The original queen of the fitness tape, Jane Fonda, helps to fuel the 1980s obsession with the body by creating a home fitness video called *Jane Fonda's Workout*.

The 1980s were all about enhancing what you had. This included breasts: the fashion called for bras that created firm, naturally shaped breasts that complemented the aerobicized physiques of the age. This in part was inspired by the rise of the modern supermodel in the shape of Cindy Crawford, Elle Macpherson, Christy Turlington and Claudia Schiffer – good, wholesome, healthy, nubile creatures whose natural-looking curves we all wanted. On the big screen, inspiration came in the fabulous form of Jamie Lee Curtis, whose athletic figure was wowing audiences in movies such as *Trading Places* (1983) and *Perfect* (1985). But, thanks to Jane Fonda and the timely proliferation of the home VCR, it was also the small screen that millions of women turned to for inspiration and motivation.

> *"My breasts are beautiful, and I gotta tell you, they've gotten a lot of attention for what is relatively short screen time."*
>
> JAMIE LEE CURTIS

CINDY CRAWFORD
Despite losing Elite's 'Look of the Year Contest' in 1982, American Cindy Crawford went on to become the most sought-after supermodel of the 1980s, appearing on the cover of over 400 magazines.

JAMIE LEE CURTIS
After starring in a succession of horror films, Jamie became known as the Queen of Scream, although films such as *Trading Places* saw her fantastic physique well and truly enter the mainstream.

Work it

Jane Fonda's video was a phenomenal success, producing a mania for dance-like exercise. Suddenly, legions of leotard-clad ladies – and the odd pert gentleman – were wearing headbands and prancing around to loud music. They boogied at the gym, in high school physical education classes and, of course, at home in front of the television screen, spurred on by Fonda. It was a simple matter of shifting the coffee table, unleashing the leotard (plus headband, wrist bands and legwarmers), backcombing the hair, putting on make-up (lots of it), and (if you had any energy left) working out! Five minutes into the workout, millions of women's thoughts turned to their breasts, which had taken on a life of their own, and a sports bra was added to a million shopping lists.

Why a sports bra?

We all know how important the right bra is when exercising – one that keeps you securely in place as you run, jump or do whatever else it is you do. First off, it's downright uncomfortable to let your breasts move around. Second, such bouncing may break down ligaments in the breasts and cause them to droop. Also, many women find the motion of their breasts embarrassing. Surprisingly, sports bras have

JANE FONDA
Throughout the 1980s, sales of Jane Fonda's fitness videos topped the bestseller lists. They were followed by a host of celebrity workout videos and new exercise techniques. Remember the 1987 hit *Calisthenics*?

CALVIN KLEIN
In 1983, Calvin Klein introduced his range of women's underwear based on his designs for men's boxers, briefs and tanks. He promoted an athletic, sporty image through his clean-cut, body-flattering styles.

Calvin Klein

only been around – at least on a significant commercial scale – since the late 1970s. Before that, women bound their breasts, or wore two or three bras at the same time, or strapped themselves into something a size too small!

The origins of the sports bra

In 1977, costume designer Hinda Miller and jogging partner Lisa Lindahl developed what they called the Jogbra. The first version was simple – two jock straps were sewn together. (Yes, jock straps. The idea came from Lindahl's husband, who waved a jock strap in the air and said 'Look, a jock bra.') First year sales were around $3,800; 12 years later they sold their company for $10 million to Playtex.

Early jogging bras worked by compressing breasts against the chest. This made exercising much more comfortable, but these bras did have at least one, very visible, drawback: they created the dreaded 'monoboob'. The fitness-conscious, body-obsessed 1980s – with its large number of workout aficionados – demanded something more flattering. So bra manufacturers went to work. Towards the mid-1980s, stronger new fabrics were developed that allowed manufacturers to create more natural silhouettes while simultaneously providing the support and stability breasts needed. Many bras began using what is known in the bra-making world as the encapsulation design. This is a design that features moulded cups, which not only support, but also separate each breast. The 1980s witnessed the dawn of the new and improved Lycra – the patron saint of all that is stretchy and comfortable – which revolutionized sports bras and workout gear. The sports bra was not only functional now, but also attractive and boldly coloured.

The sports bra and its close relative, the crop top, were soon to be seen out and about on the clubbing scene.

Brandi Chastain

Fast-forward to the end of the century, to what became the most famous sports bra to date: The year was 1999, during the year's women's soccer World Cup Final between the US and China. After kicking the game's winning goal, American Brandi Chastain dropped to her knees, pulled off her shirt and raised her arms in the air. Over her chest was a black, Nike sports bra. It was modestly cut, but sparked a frenzy of controversy (and Nike sports bra sales). Today, Chastain is a soccer coach at the University of Santa Clara in California. The sports bra is still around too, in an increasing number of colours and styles, and more popular than ever.

MODERN DESIGN
A sports bra now provides all-round support: straps that don't slip; full coverage cups; and a broad under-bust band.

Who's that girl?

Born in 1958, Madonna was the eldest daughter of eight children born to devout Catholic parents. Just five when her mother died from breast cancer, Madonna became a tireless overachiever, as well as a sexual rebel. Madonna's new stepmother was so strictly Catholic that she wouldn't allow Madonna and her sisters to wear pants with front zippers. She believed front-zipping pants were too sexually provocative. Hmmm....

Early success

Dancing was not bringing Madonna the fame she wanted. Hoping to get more attention, Madonna began performing at Manhattan nightclubs. Her strong voice, sexually charged moves and naughty clothing got her plenty of attention. In 1982, one of her admirers – DJ Mark Kamins – introduced her to the folks at Warner Brothers. They liked her, signed her and recorded her music. In 1983, Madonna's self-titled LP was released and singles *Holiday*, *Lucky Star* and *Borderline* landed in America's top 20. The rest, as they say, is history.

Career highlights

Fourteen albums, various music awards (including MTV artist, music, and video awards, Grammies, Billboard awards and American music awards), 16 films (including *Desperately Seeking Susan*, *Who's That Girl*, *Evita*), a book of naughty photographs (*Erotica*), founder of Maverick Records and author of three children's books.

In June 2004, inspired by the Kabbalah religion, Madonna announced that she wanted to change her name to 'Esther', derived from the Persian name Satarah, meaning 'star'. To husband Guy Ritchie, she is just 'Madge'.

REBELLIOUS STREAK
Renowned for her daring outfits and sexy image, Madonna not only caused a scandal due to the way she looked, but also for her outspoken views on sex, politics and religion.

Underwear as outerwear

1990

Madonna, already famous for underthings peeking out under her shirts, wears a series of stunning bras for her Blonde Ambition tour. Now it's okay to wear underwear as outerwear.

Madonna and Jean Paul Gaultier made fashion history for the way-out bra designs worn on the 1990 Blonde Ambition tour: he created them, she wore them.

A trend-setting superstar

Madonna had come to international attention in 1983 with her album *Madonna*, which she followed with records *Like a Virgin* (1984), *True Blue* (1986), and *Like a Prayer* (1989). She boosted black bra sales when she appeared in her video *Like a Virgin*, wearing said garment in a very visible way. Impressionable teens followed suit, also copying Madonna's fingerless gloves, lacy scraps and penchant for beads and crucifixes.

Underwear, outerwear or weaponry?

During the Blonde Ambition tour, she wore two corsets by Gaultier: a quilted, light pink satin creation, and one in gold. Gaultier took the 1950s 'bullet bra' as his inspiration for designing Madonna's corsets, which sport dangerous-looking conical cups combined with a faintly grandmotherly feel. An interesting combination! The huge media frenzy surrounding the Diva's dress, or lack thereof, truly brought the corset back to the forefront of fashion. For the same tour Gaultier also designed a black studded bra for her, which later brought $14,000 at auction. According to the late Frederick Mellinger, Madonna was good for business. Her Blonde Ambition tour helped boost fashion bra and corset sales by 40 per cent at Frederick's of Hollywood,

PRETTY PENNY
In 2001, Madonna's black-beaded Dolce and Gabbana bra sold for $23,850 in an online auction.

estimated Mellinger, the company's owner and founder. Madonna and Fredericks go way back. The lingerie giant furnished some of the costumes for the pop star's Blonde Ambition tour, and the singer returned the favour by donating used brassieres to the store's museum. After one $10,000 model was stolen (security is much better these days), Madonna simply sent over another.

Expensive underwear

Apparently, Madonna's bras are popular auction items. While most go for around $10,000, many bring in quite a penny more. For instance, a Jean Paul Gaultier-designed, black and fuschia number worn on the Blonde Ambition tour brought in $21,150. Who would pay that for a bra? Why, the Museum of Fashion and Textiles in Santiago, Chile, of course. The biggest money-maker has been a black-beaded Dolce and Gabbana number from The Girlie Tour that fetched $23,850 from a private collector in a recent online auction. Another bra – black with gold tassels from the Who's That Girl tour – went for $20,550. Makes you wonder what a pair of Madge's knickers would go for?

A bra or a car?

Thierry Mugler, too, has long been a great proponent of the corset, and during the late 1980s and early 1990s came out with some truly original designs such as his 1989 'Built like a Buick' and the 1990 'Diver'. Not entirely suitable for a quick trip to the supermarket. The greatest thing about corsets is their element of risqué through associations with the fetishist movement, which drives some men wild, while making the wearer feel powerful and sexy. Their design elements have since been used in evening gowns to great effect by the dresses of Christian LaCroix, John Galliano, Versace and Karl Lagerfield. Interestingly, corset design is often featured in wedding dresses, making an ironic combination of that which is exotic and erotic with the pure.

> *"I stand for freedom of expression, doing what you believe in, and going after your dreams."*
>
> MADONNA

THE TOURS ...

THE VIRGIN TOUR
Tickets for Madonna's first fully-fledged tour sold out within hours. Although the catchy pop songs and sexy image were a hit with fans, many critics weren't so impressed, predicting that she would sink without trace within six months.

WHO'S THAT GIRL
Madonna's first world tour in 1987 took her to eight different countries. Riot police had to be called in Japan to calm thousands of distraught teenagers when a concert had to be cancelled after a severe storm.

BLONDE AMBITION
This controversial 1990 tour remains the most talked about ever. The incorporated themes of sex and religion caused problems all over the world, especially in Italy, where the Pope called for a boycott of all shows.

Jean Paul Gaultier

Born in Paris in 1952, Gaultier's career highlight was undoubtedly costuming for the Blonde Ambition tour. Interestingly, the real life clothing he created during this period mimicked the conical bras and corsets worn by Madonna and her crew. Gaultier went on to create a number of fragrances – Classique, Summer Fragrance – housed in bottles the shape of women's torsos. The breasts were conical as well, and often dressed in bras or corsets. He is currently head designer at Hermes, his first experience as a head designer for a company other than his own.

'Putting a skirt on a man is not a travesty. Putting a bra on him is,' was Jean Paul Gaultier's answer when questioned about the male skirts he often designs. (For the record, Gaultier also put men in bras – just have a look at some of Madonna's back-up dancers on her Blonde Ambition tour.) In 2001, Gaultier won France's Legion of Honour, presented by his first fashion employer, Pierre Cardin.

GIRLIE SHOW
The most extravagant of Madonna's outings, during which the cast wore a total of 1,500 costumes. The 1993 tour caused more controversy, especially in Puerto Rico, after Madonna rubbed the country's flag between her legs.

Return of the waif

1993

Kate Moss appears in British *Vogue* modelling underwear. The pictures show a hollow-chested, rail-thin Kate looking far from glamorous, and cause an international furore.

With their skin-and-bone frames, barely there breasts, gaunt faces, plucked eyebrows, and vacuous looks, the waif models personified the grunge and heroin chic fashion movements of the early 1990s.

Thin is in

The definition of a waif from *Webster's New Collegiate Dictionary* is: 'a stray person or animal; esp. a homeless child'. The waifs of the early 1990s weren't strays, nor were they homeless, though some might argue they looked like children!

The waif had returned. Only unlike Twiggy, the original waif, the new waif looked to all intents and purposes sick and strung out. The image of extreme thinness and frailty was widely criticized for encouraging young girls to develop eating disorders in an effort to achieve the bodies of the most famous models of that time. Calvin Klein, who just a few years earlier had introduced his sporty, athletic bras and pants, found himself at the centre of a media frenzy surrounding the new heroin chic and the bony Ms Moss.

Sleek comfort

The bold colours and opulence of the 1980s were out of the picture. Androgyny was in, and unisex clothing in black, white and grey was all the rage. Clothing styles weren't particularly tailored, body-conscious or bust-oriented, so women needed bras that felt good and held their assets in place while creating a natural silhouette. Emphasis was on barely there underwear; anything too uplifting, padded or cleavage-creating would look strange under the period's clothing. Seamless bras, which were comfortable and gave a sleek line under T-shirts and tank tops, became increasingly popular. Bras in colours other than white and beige were favourites with younger women, and it was common to see black, pink, or red bra straps peeking out from tank tops. It was a tantalizing hint at a woman's sexuality – not an all-out assault like the later Wonderbra would create.

KATE MOSS
Although this London-born model found fame through her skinniness, she has retained her popularity – and put on a little weight?

GRUNGE PERSONIFIED
Singer Courtney Love has become known as the queen of chic grunge, with her bras always visible, and her devil-may-care attitude.

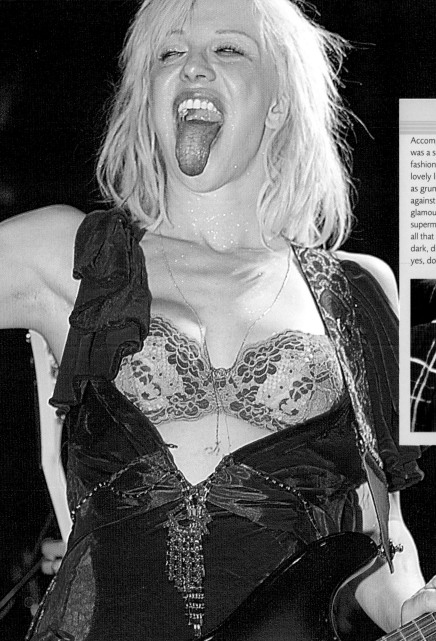

Grunge

Accompanying the waif look was a somewhat depressing fashion trend (with relation to lovely lingerie anyway), known as grunge. As a direct reaction against the perfection and glamour of the 1980s supermodels, grunge embodied all that was shabby, shoddy, dark, dirty, dishevelled and yes, downright depressing.

Va-va-va voom!

1994

'Hello Boys I'm Back.' The cleavage makes a spectacular return and the bra battles begin with Wonderbra in one corner, and Gossard's Ultrabra in the other.

In the midst of waifs, grunge and the like, came the Wonderbra. Strange timing, but apparently there were enough non-waif women who desired glamazon breasts that one Wonderbra sold every 15 seconds in the US alone.

Origins of Wonderbra

We think of the Wonderbra as a modern garment, yet there was a Wonder Bra – two words – in the 1940s. Produced by a US-based company called d'Amour Foundations, the patented bra featured an inverted v-shape insert between the strap and cup. This gave the wearer greater flexibility in adjusting her bra, allowing her to lift breasts to greater heights.

BRA OF THE CENTURY?
Sexy, seductive and supportive, the Wonderbra was the definitive modern bra.

The Wonderbra as we now know it was designed back in 1964 by the French designer Louise Poirier, but did not explode onto the bra market until an article in 1992 in British *Vogue* raved about the push-up and plunge bra. Shortly thereafter Gossard claimed to be selling 22,000 Wonderbras a week.

Battle of the bras

However, Gossard's license to produce the Wonderbra expired – ouch! – and the product was snapped up by Playtex (a division of Sara Lee), who relaunched Wonderbra with their already legendary, high-profile ad campaign using the obvious charms of the ultra-gorgeous Eva Herzigova.

BILLBOARD ADVERTS

PULLING POWER
The Wonderbra's amazing 'pulling power' was graphically illustrated by fabulous billboard displays like this one. The phenomenally successful ad campaign helped to create such high demand for cleavage-enhancing bras that the bra industry as a whole was given a boost. Many of the Wonderbra ads were hailed as instant classics.

> *"It's called the 'Sheep Dog Bra'... It rounds them up and points them in the right direction."*
>
> *ANON*

EVA HERZIGOVA

Eva Herzigova was named the 'face' of Wonderbra and appeared on the enormous 2,800 square foot billboard in Times Square, New York. The hugely successful ad campaign, 'Hello Boys', caused sales to soar, with the US store Macey's reputedly selling a staggering 3,000 bras every day.

ADRIANA SKLENARIKOVA

Born in Czechoslovakia, Adriana is best known in Europe, where she represents Wonderbra and Peroni Beer. She married the French soccer star Christian Karembeu and is now Adriana Sklenarikova Karembeu – quite a mouthful!

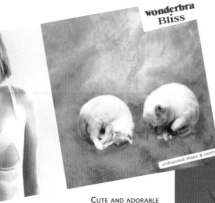

wonderbra
Bliss

CUTE AND ADORABLE
Wonderbra offers another style of
padded underwired bra with plunging neckline and
trademark uplift. The kittens look great too.

> *"I swear, even
> I get cleavage
> with them."*
>
> KATE MOSS (ON THE WONDERBRA)

Suddenly everyone wanted cleavage, and Wonderbra was the way to get it. Spurred on by increasing fears over the danger of silicone implants, the population (female) turned towards their bras for those added breast inches. The thoroughly sexy Wonderbra hit New York stores in May 1994 amidst a storm of excitement usually reserved for celebrities. The boxes of bras were transported across New York by limousines accompanied by 'secret-service' men and models in dark glasses and yellow Wonderbra baseball hats. In Miami they arrived in pink Cadillacs, in San Francisco by cable car, and in Los Angeles they were flown in by helicopter. Wonderbras sold at an incredible rate, and first year sales of the bra were estimated to be $120 million in the US alone.

Gossard's scheme

The folks at Gossard knew Playtex's grand American plans for the Wonderbra. To compete, the British company moved quickly to launch its own version of the Wonderbra – called the Super-Uplift bra (it was the Ultrabra in the UK) ahead of the Wonderbra. The scheme worked. In stores in March 1994, right around the time pre-publicity was appearing for the not-yet-launched Wonderbra, Gossard took advantage of consumers' collective excitement. Women visited the

BOOB JOB £19

super*boost*
BY *Gossard*

AS SEEN IN HOUSE OF FRASER AND OTHER LEADING DEPARTMENT STORES

'BIGGEST CLEAVAGE EVER...OR YOUR MONEY BACK'
This is how Gossard marketed their Superboost bra, launched in 2001 with the help of Emma Griffiths. It was an instant success, and the first time that a cleavage-enhancing bra was made available in larger sizes, going up to a F cup.

Not rocket science?

The Wonderbra is a miracle of modern science and precision engineering at its best. The bra features 54 design elements making it one of the most complicated articles of clothing to produce. The cups alone are constructed with three parts, not to mention the precision angled back and underwired cups with removable pads called 'cookies'.

department store only to find the Wonderbra was months away from arriving. Not wanting to leave empty-handed, they bought Gossard's Super-Uplift bra, a $46 bra that was a full $20 more expensive than Playtex's version. 'Truly the Original Super Uplift Push Up from England,' the bra's hang tags said. The strategy worked, and Gossard averaged $100,000 in bra sales in one week. By May, Gossard had already sold $8 million worth of bras and expected to reach $20 million by year's end, almost ten times its original estimate. Ultimately, though, the Ultrabra never quite reached the sales of the Wonderbra.

Joining the party

The other major bra manufacturers all joined in the fun. Victoria's Secret brought out their hugely successful Miracle Bra, Maidenform produced the Rendezvous, Wacoal had the Push-Up bra and Vanity Fair introduced their It Must Be Magic bra.

Susan Malinowsi, then Vice President of Marketing at Maidenform, noted: 'Wonderbra helped create demand that it can't possibly fill, so women are looking at every single push-up and plunge bra out there. The rest of us are enjoying a phenomenal free ride.'

IT'S A MIRACLE!
Victoria's Secret brought out their own sexy push-up bra in the shape of the Miracle Bra, here modelled by Karen Mulder.

Million-dollar bras

1996

Victoria's Secret rings in the 1996 holiday season with its first Fantasy Bra. With over 100 carat's worth of diamonds, it goes on sale at a jaw-dropping $1 million.

Each year Victoria's Secret features a different-style bra (strapless, push-up and so on), different rocks (one year straight diamonds, another pink sapphires or rubies), and a one-of-a-kind name (Diamond Dream Bra and Heavenly Star Bra). Oh, and each year a different supermodel gets the honour of wearing the bejewelled bra in the company's holiday catalogue and during its much-publicized fashion show. Past honours have gone to Claudia Schiffer, Tyra Banks, Heidi Klum and Gisele Bundchen.

Pure fantasy

Yes, these are fabulous pieces of lingerie. However, with prices moving upwards of $10 million, one wonders: have any sold? Not yet. Seems a lot of people contact Victoria's Secret about the bras, but in the end, these gorgeous pieces are simply pure fantasy.

1997

Victoria's Secret faces a unique challenge: how to top the previous year's million-dollar offering? The answer? Make an even more expensive Fantasy Bra! Victoria's Secret commissioned Harry Winston to decorate a strapless push-up bra with three million dollars' worth of diamonds, including 100 pear-shaped stones (total weight 93 carats), 99 smaller diamonds for the trim, and a 42-carat pear-shaped diamond for the décolletage.

1998

This is the year of the breathtaking $5 million Dream Angels Bra, modelled by the Czech supermodel, Daniela Pestova. Based on Victoria's Secret Angel push-up bra, it is the most romantic of the Fantasy Bras. It is adorned with 77 carats of marquise-shaped rubies and 330 carats of pear and marquise-shaped diamonds, all set in platinum, which decorate the top of the cups, décolletage and straps. The total 600 glittering gems are arranged in a delicate floral pattern. Heavenly!

1999

The world has millennium fever so is it any surprise that Victoria's Secret's holiday 1999 bra is called the Millennium Bra? To further celebrate the new century, the bra features 2,000 diamonds and blue sapphires set in platinum.

What's the secret?

Who knows? Though the company doesn't admit it, the name could refer to our 19th century matriarch, Queen Victoria. Rumours abound about a lusty, late-in-life secret affair with one of her servants. British bluebloods having illicit affairs ... surely not!

"The most glamorous Christmas gift ever."

BILLING FOR FANTASY BRA

Heidi's hat trick

In 2003, Victoria's Secret supermodel Heidi Klum was chosen for the third time to be the face (and breasts) of the company's prestigious advertising campaign, which collectively has earned her more than $40 million! Heidi also modelled the 1999 $10 million Millennium Bra and the 2001 $12.5 million Heavenly Star Bra.

The Very Sexy Fantasy Bra

• The 2003 fantasy bra, designed by Mouawad, featured the 70-carat Excelsior Diamond .This pear-shaped stone was cut from the second-largest rough diamond ever found in the world.

• The triangle bra and panty set, worth $11 million, paid tribute to Broadway, resembling the bright lights of Broadway's Marquis Theatre.

• It is created with a combination of orange and yellow sapphires, garnets and amethysts, surrounded by diamonds.

• The bra alone comprises 2,809 stones and weighs a total of 2,200 carats. The panty contributes an additional 3,236 stones.

• Over 375 hours of labour went into the construction of this original lingerie design, making it one of the most labour-intensive creations Victoria's Secret has ever produced.

Oh, and to really reinforce the millennial theme, one of the straps spells out '2000' in gemstones. Modelled by Heidi Klum and available for $10 million US.

2000

The Red Hot Fantasy Bra is a bikini-style bra laden with – what else? – rubies. A mere 300 carats of Thai rubies, a few semi-precious stones and a handful of diamonds. Priced at a cool $15 million, it is modelled by Gisele Bundchen. (No, Victoria's Secret doesn't let the models keep these things.)

STAR OF THE SHOW
Heidi Klum got to shine a second time, becoming the only model to live the fantasy twice when she modelled the 2001 Heavenly Star Bra. This exquisite bra is adorned with more than 2,000 diamonds.

2001

For this year's Fantasy offering, Victoria's Secret reaches out to famed jewellery house, Mouawad, for help. The result of the collaboration is the $12.5 million Heavenly Star Bra. (Don't you wonder who is responsible for naming these things?) Modelled by Heidi Klum, the demi-cup brassiere is adorned with 1,200 pink sapphires and more than 2,300 round and marquise diamonds. The finishing touch? A 90-carat flawless diamond nestled right between the cups. A piece of Victoria Secret trivia is in order: With the wearing of the Heavenly Star Bra, Heidi Klum earns the illustrious title of 'Only Victoria's Secret Model to Wear a Fantasy Bra Twice'. Another interesting bit: This is the first year a Fantasy Bra has cost less than the version preceding it.

2002

The trend continues: This year's Fantasy Bra costs less than the one before. It's also, just like the year before, designed by Mouawad. Inspired by the curvy lines of Victoria's Secret's Very Sexy Bra, The Star of Victoria Bra, priced at $10 million, features 1,150 ruby 'roses' and 1,600 emerald 'leaves'. Plus, there's a 60-carat, pear-shaped diamond right at the cleavage. Modelled by Karolina Kurkova. No one splashes out on this one, either.

C

The ɡ　　　　ʜas
workeᵈ　　　　's
Secret o.　　　ʟsʏ
Bras. Best　　　ᵣ
the 2003 O.
given special
bra and pantie.
Secret, customiz
with a pair of $5,0
convertible into a n
made of white gold and
22 diamonds.

The Shape of Things to Come

A few short years into the new millennium, bras today represent form, function and fun. There are shape-shifting minimizers for the abundant, padded push-ups for the petite, tough athletic bras for sports, cleavage-enhancing bras for seduction and confections in all manners of fabrics, colours and cuts with no purpose but sheer delight.

But bras are getting clever too. Now even able to screen for cancer, your lingerie will lift, support and enhance your life like never before.

F *2000+*

The corset comeback

2001

High-style musical *Moulin Rouge* hits the big screen. The seductive costumes and sensational style of the box-office smash reignites a long-forgotten trend for corsets.

Director Baz Luhrmann's musical extravaganza is a sumptuous celebration of 20th century music in the dazzling, if anachronistic, setting of Paris and Montmartre, in France's most notorious nightclub the Moulin Rouge. The song and dance is breathtaking and exuberant but it is the gorgeous colour and costumes that really steal the show.

MODERN-DAY MOULIN
Former principal dancer at the real Moulin Rouge, Marissa Burgess proves that the sumptuous costumes are still as lavish as ever.

LES FOLIES BERGÈRE
When Paris's original dance hall opened in 1869, its daring costumes and beautiful dancers made it the toast of European high society.

The bodice is back

The movie proved that although Hollywood may have had its golden age a long time ago, it can still have a huge influence on fashion. Inspired by the sexy bodice worn by Nicole Kidman, who starred as the tragic courtesan Satine in the blockbuster movie, bra manufacturers rolled out new lines of wasp-waisted one-pieces that would not have looked out of place on a poster by the diminutive French artist Toulouse Lautrec (who loved to hang out at the Moulin Rouge painting the dancing girls and supping absinthe). Lingerie fashion at the turn of the 21st century was barely discernable from lingerie fashion at the turn of the 20th century.

Belle époque

The names of the new lines took up the theme: Cabaret, Montmartre, Belle Epoque and, inevitably, Moulin Rouge. The French lingerie company Barbara led the way, manufacturing elegant Swiss-embroidered corsets decorated with starry polka dots. Gossard unleashed their Ultrabra Cancan, a black Chantilly lace number decorated with red satin bows. Although clearly harking back to a bygone era, the products were designed very much with the modern woman in mind, using lightweight fabrics. A spokeswoman for Gossard enthused, 'The Moulin Rouge is a clear inspiration for the collection. We are looking back to a time of mythic cabaret, the exuberance and, of course, the look created by Nicole Kidman. The inspiration is historical but the line we have created is thoroughly modern.'

A MOMENT IN TIME
Toulouse Lautrec was often seen sketching in the Moulin Rouge, capturing both intimate moments and dramatic dance scenes.

NICOLE KIDMAN
Kidman's Golden Globe-winning performance influenced the 2002 Paris Lingerie Fair, giving it a distinctly turn-of-the-twentieth-century feel.

LADY OF LUXURY
21st century corsets are luxurious and lightweight, like this Lady Marlene design from Gelmart.

BRA DIVA
We can't keep her out of our head or out of our lingerie drawers. Kylie has become a sex goddess and bra diva in one. She's pretty under-whelmed by her own image, however, describing herself as a 'drag queen caught in a woman's body', declaring: 'I'm not sexy'. But thankfully for her bra sales, very few of us believe that.

Stars and their bras

2003

Petite Aussie singer/actress Kylie Minogue features in an erotic advert for Agent Provocateur's lingerie. The cinema-only advertisement causes a furore.

In the sensational ad, Kylie exploits every ounce of her considerable sex appeal as she cavorts in full suspender-clad regalia upon a bucking bronco (surely not simulating seriously raunchy sex?). The tabloids went wild and the Agent Provocateur commercial won 'Best Cinema Commercial of the Year' at the British TV Awards.

Love Kylie

Kylie flaunts and taunts with that dance-toned body, the music almost secondary to the main event. Kylie might be truly famous for her singing and fabulous bottom, but it seems we find her chest pretty inspiring too. So much so that Kylie was voted

LOVEABLE LINGERIE
Pop princess and sexy screen siren Kylie also designs her own lingerie, LoveKylie, a range of 'elegant boudoir styles with beautiful fabrics, sleek design and flirtatious detailing'.

the sexiest pop pin-up in the world by viewers of music channel VH1. Our vote of confidence in the Aussie pop princess's *Rhythm of Love* has been boosted further still by the runaway success of LoveKylie, her own brand of lingerie, launched in Selfridges to a massive media frenzy and incredible sales. Demand for the diminutive one's designer smalls far exceeded supply, with Selfridges having to double their orders to cope. *Hand on Your Heart* – or should that be bra? Who can resist Kylie's ever-expanding assets?

> "It's all an image, it's not reality."
>
> *KYLIE MINOGUE*

The body

Of course, gorgeous Kylie isn't the only one cashing in on the cleavage ticket. Other singers, actresses and models (most of whom have already made millions from their other pursuits) are cashing in on the 'x' factor of their own brand bras.

Referred to as 'The Body' in her native Australia, Elle Macpherson's amazing six-foot frame has graced enough magazine covers to secure her a place as one of the original supermodels. Elle has been in the lingerie game since 1990. Now she doesn't even need to model her sumptuous wares herself, stepping firmly behind the camera as the brand's creative director. 'The Body' has become 'The Entrepreneur', with the former Victoria's Secret model grooming her Elle Macpherson Intimates range into a $10 million international enterprise.

Maternity bras

Elle Macpherson's home life revolves around her two children – and, unsurprisingly, Elle revamped the maternity bra so that she, and the buying public, can look good when feeding junior.

There have been patents for nursing bras since the late 1800s. However, the garments weren't widely used until the late 1960s when breastfeeding became fashionable (thanks to a push towards natural living) and women, who during the previous decades had given up nursing in favour of manufactured baby formula, began breastfeeding in greater numbers. Today, most mainstream bra brands make a nursing bra, as do specialty nursing wear clothing lines and

ELLE MACPHERSON **INTIMATES**
Photographer: Regan Cameron
Date: 70593
Sheet No: 28968

ELLE
Launched in 1990, Elle's Intimates range is now an internationally renowned lingerie company, with Elle still very much at the helm.

MATERNELLE
It's never going to be the sexiest item of lingerie, but the maternity bra has come a long way since the 1800s, reaching an elegant peak with Elle's Intimates' Maternelle bras.

"Underwear is such an emotional thing."

ELLE MACPHERSON

maternity lines. These are available in a wide range of colours, sizes and styles – from racy-styled seducers to heavy-duty support models – and incorporate many of the same elements of everyday fashion bras. It's hard to believe that nursing bras were once classified as medical sundries to be manufactured by medical supply companies.

The brain

A secret to Elle's success has been the clever licensing of her image that appeals to women and men. As a brand, Elle Macpherson has extended herself to include a line of sportswear and intimate apparel for Montgomery Ward. Not to mention that string of Fashion Cafés. And she can act. Elle's film credits include parts in: *Sirens*, *Alice*, *Jane Eyre*, *If Lucy Fell*, *The Mirror Has Two Faces*, *Batman & Robin* and *The Edge*. It seems that being a celebrity bra icon has more to do with brain power than cup size, aboard the cleavage express ride to fame and fortune.

Caprice

Although she has graced over 250 magazine covers, often leaving little to the imagination, Caprice is more than just a pair of breasts and a pretty face. In 2001 she launched the aptly named best-selling lingerie range, Caprice, and, as well as having a list of credits in films, theatre and TV, has just lent her name to the Caprice Hair Straighteners.

A PRETTY FACE
Caprice has been voted the sexiest women in the world, but behind the sultry facade lies an apparently astute business woman, not afraid to turn her hand to anything that comes her way.

Bizarre bras

2004

One hundred years after Charles De Bevoise first named the revolutionary 'brassiere', the bra joins the fight against breast cancer and establishes itself as a girl's new best friend.

At the turn of the 20th century, the bra was hailed as a 'lifesaver' when it freed us from the confines of the corset. In 2004 it is once again hailed as lifesaver – this time literally!

Bionic bras

Just how brainy are bras nowadays? Well, smart enough to let you know if you have a malignant tumour growing in your breast. Researchers from the De Montfort University in Leicester, in the UK, have designed a bra that is hailed to be a huge breakthrough in breast screening. The technology is claimed to be as effective as X-ray mammograms, while being cheaper, safer and quicker to read. The 'Smart Bra' is fitted with a microchip that registers the difference between healthy breast tissue and malignant growths. Tiny electrical currents are passed through the breast, and in areas where the current's passage is different from normal, the chip is able to determine a problem.

ANTI-SMOKING BRA
The floral scent emitted by this bra is designed to stop women having cigarette cravings.

Walk the Walk

In November 1996, Briton Nina Barough had no experience of fundraising or marathons; however, she and 13 women decided to powerwalk the New York Marathon in their bras, raising £25,000 for breast cancer research.

In 1997 Nina discovered a tumour in her own breast and her fundraising took on a new meaning. In 1998 Walk the Walk became an official charity and the first Moonwalk was held on the eve of the London Marathon, starting at midnight and finishing at seven the next morning. The night was a huge success and the Moonwalk is now a major annual event, attracting a host of celebrities including Nell MacAndrew, Victoria Wood and Lorraine Kelly.

MOONWALK WARM-UP 2004
Sponsored by Playtex since November 1998, The Moonwalk is the only powerwalking marathon in the world at present and the only marathon where practically all entrants, male and female, wear bras!

Incredible edible undies

What's a girl's best friend after our diamonds and our bras?
Yes, it's out there – the first 100 per cent chocolate bra
designed by Reinlinde Trummer. All we need now is for
Victoria's Secret to take up the idea, add a few diamonds and
we really will have the ultimate fantasy bra! Trummer uses a
special chocolate that apparently doesn't melt (at least not
at body temperature), so if things should get heated when
wearing one of the bras, in theory they shouldn't let you down
at the wrong moment. They are works of art in their own right
with elaborate floral designs. Each bra needs at least two kilos
of chocolate to make, and may have pepper, chilli and
whisky added for a little extra buzz.

Wow!

But if you think chocolate bras are bizarre, take a trip
to the antipodes, home of the World of Wearable
Art Awards (WOW) that takes place annually
in Nelson, New Zealand. A highlight of
the show is the Bizarre Bra competition,
which is an amalgam of art, theatre
and fashion, and the inspiration for
some of the most extraordinary bras
imaginable. For example, there's the
Violingerie Bra, which is made of
fake fur and adorned with small
violins that actually play tunes!

THE BUDGIE BRA
One Bizarre Bra competition winner
was the Budgerigar Brassiere. Emily
Bullock created this bra out of the
stuffed bodies of her two favourite
budgies, which had passed on. If
that's not bizarre...

BRA OF CHOCOLATE
Made from special
chocolate, this
delicious bra is
guaranteed not to
melt in the heat of
the moment.

A bra that fits: finding your perfect size

A poll in Britain's *Prima* magazine found that only 38 per cent of men knew the correct size of their partner's bra. However, before you start tutting, it's worth noting that over 60 per cent of women do not know their own correct bra size!

Finding your best fit

Fortunately, a good-fitting brassiere is possible. Here's a classic formula for finding your best fit:

- Use a measuring tape – the kind found in a sewing kit, not the type buried in a tool box.
- Enlist help. Your measurements will be more accurate if someone else takes them. If that's not possible, begin by facing a full-length mirror.
- Measuring against bare skin will give you the most

accurate results. If someone else is taking your numbers and you're feeling shy, don a tight-fitting seamless T-shirt over bare breasts.

- There are two elements to your bra size: the band size (ie 32, 34, 36) and cup size (ie A, B, C). Start with the band size, also called frame size. Wrap the measuring tape tightly around your ribcage, just below your bust. Add 5 inches to the measurement. Thus, a ribcage measurement of 27in + 5in would equal a 32in band size.
- Find your cup size: measure loosely around the fullest part of your bust. Subtract your band size from this measurement. A difference of 1in=A cup, 2in=B cup, 3in=C cup, 4in=D cup. For example, a cup measurement of 34in–32in band size equals 2in, or a B cup.
- Be prepared to re-measure every few years. Breasts change size with time, which is why bra-fitting experts recommend re-evaluating your measurements at least once every two years – more often if you've lost or gained a significant amount of weight or had a baby.

Little or large?

If you're large-breasted you will need extra support from your bra. If your breasts are very small, your bra can give you a boost.

- Large-busted? Go with an underwire, full-coverage bra. Not only are full-coverage styles more comfortable for the full-figured, they are more flattering. Look also for wide straps, which are less likely to dig in to your skin.
- Small-busted? If you'd like to look bustier, try a padded bra, a cleavage-enhancing bra or a demi-bra which can lift breasts and enhance cleavage. These types of bras are now more widely available than ever.

Cup-size variations

The United States, United Kingdom and continental Europe have slightly different systems for super-sized bra cups. Americans move from A, B, C and D to DD, DDD, E, F and FF cups. The British prefer to go from A, B, C, D to DD and then E, F, to FF and then G. The Continental Europeans take a more straightforward approach, moving straight up the alphabet from A, B, C, D, E, F, G and H to I.

Perils of a bad bra

You'll know a bad bra when you wear one – it is uncomfortable, unflattering and shows under clothing. But a bad bra is more than just a nuisance, it can also affect your health:

- Years of wearing a bra with overly-tight straps can cause permanent indentations in the top of the shoulders.
- A bad bra can cause chronic upper back, neck, and shoulder pain. In some instances, an ill-fitting bra can even contribute to headaches.
- An ill-fitting bra can lead to pain during exercise. Apart from the danger of sagging breasts over time, bras can chafe the skin during exercise. A specially designed bra can increase your comfort and so improve your performance.
- Itchy material, poorly designed cups, bands and straps can cause skin abrasions even when you are not exercising.
- To sum up, if you are very conscious of your bra while you are wearing it, it's probably not a well-fitting bra.

Get it right

Are you wearing the correct bra size? Get online and log onto one of the following websites. Better still, get yourself professionally fitted at a reputable store.

- www.afraidtoask.com/breast/brasizeform1.html
- www.breasttalk.co.uk/bra_size_calculator.htm (a great site that helps you find American, European and UK sizes)
- www.lovableusa.com/calc-bra.jsp
- www.grandstyle.com/cloth07.htm (includes tips for special bra-fitting issues and concerns, such as asymmetrical breasts).

Index

Acknowledgments

Author's acknowledgment: Writing a book is a group effort – this one, especially, has been so! I couldn't have finished "The Bra Book" without the following people: my husband Richard Demler and our sons L.C. Pedersen and A.G. Pedersen, all of whom provided moral support; Pearl Garcia Wiliams for watching over my family, my home and me so I could write; Nancy Bloom and Carla Hall for love, laughter, good meals and support; the incredibly talented and oh, so, patient folks at Studio Cactus; and to you, dear reader, for your interest.

Studio Cactus would like to thank: Wonderbra and Playtex (Sara Lee Intimates), Victoria's Secret, Mouawad, Frederick's of Hollywood, Gelmart Industries, Triumph International, Maidenform Inc, Bendon and Elle Macpherson Intimates for their invaluable contributions to this project. Many thanks, too, to Robert Opie. Special thanks to Lucinda Hawksley, Tam Pickeral and Victoria Harwood for their expert contributions to the text and to Aisling Culhane for modelling. Thanks to Kate Hawkins and Claire Moore for their illustrations; Sharon Moore, Laura Watson and Dawn Terrey for design; Clare Wallis and Ame Verso for their expert editing; Lorna Hankin and Emily Hawkins for editorial assistance; Polly Boyd for proofreading; Phil Carré, Will Jones, Sharon Rudd and Claire Moore for Photoshop work; Helen Stallion and Julia Harris-Voss for picture research; and Zeb Korycinska for the indexing. As always, special thanks to Madeleine and Jacky.

Picture credits

Every effort has been made to trace the copyright holders; we apologize in advance for any unintentional omissions. We will be pleased to insert the appropriate acknowledgement in any subsequent edition of this publication.

Abbreviations: t = top; b = bottom; c = centre; l = left; r = right.

Courtesy of The Advertising Archive: 9(bl), 41(l,r), 44–45, 50(r), 51(t), 55, 60–61, 66(l), 67, 86(r), 94(l,r), 98, 108(b), 118, 119, 120(t); akg-images: 46(r), 48(b); akg-images/Cameraphoto: 22(b), 54(r); Album/akg-images: 97(l,r); Maximillian Weinzierl/Alamy: 123(l); Popperfoto/Alamy: 14(r), 64(br); The Art Archive/Bibliothèque des Arts Décoratifs Paris/Dagli Orti: 20(t); The Art Archive/Dagli Orti: 16–17, 19; The Art Archive/Galleria degli Uffizi Florence/Dagli Orti: 23; The Art Archive/HeraklionMuseum/Dagli Orti: 18(l,c); The Art Archive/Musée d'Art et d'Historie Metz/Dagli Orti: 25(t); The Art Archive/Musée de Louvre, Paris/Dagli Orti: 18(tr); British Film Institute: 13(cl), 89; Archives Larousse/Giraudon/Bridgeman: 38; Bibliothèque des Arts Décoratifs, Paris, France/www.bridgeman.co.uk: 34(l), 37, 47(r), 87(c); Bibliothèque Nationale, Paris, France/www.bridgeman.co.uk: 28; 35; Bibliothèque Municipale, Rouen, France/www.bridgeman.co.uk: 20(b); Chateau de Loches, France/www.bridgeman.co.uk: 21; Louvre, Paris, France/www.bridgeman.co.uk: 34(r); Mucha Trust/www.bridgeman.co.uk: 8(t); Private Collection/www.bridgeman.co.uk: 22(t), 87(r); David Steen/Camera Press: 82; ©Bettman/CORBIS: 27, 29(r), 53(br), 58(r), 64(bl), 65(l,r), 69(b), 72(bl), 83(l), 84, 110(b); ©CinemaPhoto/CORBIS: 68(br), 73(tl); Corbis Images: 11(tr); ©CORBIS: 35(r) 63(l); ©Historical Picture Archive/CORBIS: 24(r); ©Hulton-Deutsch Collection/Corbis: 36, 46(l), 62(l), 63(r); ©John Springer Collection/CORBIS: 74(br); ©Lorenzo Ciniglio/CORBIS: 105(l); ©Neil Preston/CORBIS: 100, 101, 102(l,br), 103(r,t), 105(r); ©NINIO DORYL/CORBIS SYGMA: 116(b); ©Peter Harholdt/CORBIS: 117(tl); ©Pierre Vauthey/CORBIS SYGMA: 95(t,b); ©rien/CORBIS SYGMA: 96(l); ©Roger Ressmeyer/CORBIS: 102(bl); ©SUNSET BOULEVARD/CORBIS SYGMA: 68(l), 74(bl), 77; ©Strauss/Curtis/CORBIS: 88; ©Studio Patellani/CORBIS: 72(br); ©Swim Ink/CORBIS: 29(l), 116(c); ©Underwood & Underwood/CORBIS: 47(l), 49(l); ©Dover: 8(bl), 30–31; Elle Macpherson Intimates for Bendon Ltd, all rights reserved: 120(l,b); ©Frederick's of Hollywood: 9(br), 15(bc), 74(t), 76(l), 77(b); Gelmart: 13(c), 86(l), 87(bl); Archive Photos/Getty Images: 43(br); BIPs/Getty Images: 42(r); Carlo Bavagnoli/Getty Images: 85(b); Central Press/Hulton Getty: 59(r); Getty Images: 33(t); Henry Guttmann/Getty Images: 49(r); John Kobal Foundation/Getty Images: 48(c); Keystone/Getty Images: 70, 85(t); Pat English/Getty Images: 71(t); Picture Post/Getty Images: 15(r); Vechio/Getty: 73(br); Keystone Archive: 39(c); 20th Century Fox/The Kobal Collection: 117(b,l); MGM/The Kobal Collection/Laszlo Willinger: 56; Paramount/The Kobal Collection: 54(l); Polygram/The Kobal Collection/Clive Coote: 10(cr); RKO/The Kobal Collection/George Hurrell: 66(br); RKO/The Kobal Collection: 66(cr); Spelling/ABC/The Kobal Collection: 95(l); United Artists/The Kobal Collection: 32(l); Maidenform Inc: 8(bc), 52, 53(c); Mary Evans Picture Library: 33(b), 42(l), 68(tr); Victoria's Secret and Mouawad USA, Inc: 110, 111(l), 112, 113; National Archives: 40(l), 62(r); PA Photos: 104, 109, 121, 123(r); Playtex for Sarah Lee Intimates: 66(tr); Rex Features: 43(t), 90(t), 91, 96(r); Robert Opie: 8(br), 57, 83(b); Science Museum/Science and Society Picture Library: 25(b), 26(b); Topham Picturepoint: 76(r); ©Triumph International, 2004, Munich, all rights reserved: 10(l), 12(l), 13(r), 14(l), 93, 99(r), 114-115, 117(r), 122(l); US Patent Office: 32(r); Vintage Magazine Co.: 80(l,r), 81(l,r); Walk the Walk: 122(r); Wonderbra for Sara Lee Intimates: 9(bc), 11(tr,br), 106(c,b), 107(r,b), 108(l); Zefa/Retrofile: 78–79.

Artwork: Claire Moore: 50(l); Kate Hawkins: 18(l), 24(l), 26(t), 39(l), 40(tr), 72(c). **Additional photography**: Damien Moore: 1, 12, 90. **Jacket:** Bettmann/CORBIS.